570

ACPL ITEM
DISCARDED

D1601291

**DO NOT REMOVE
CARDS FROM POCKET**

ALLEN COUNTY PUBLIC LIBRARY

FORT WAYNE, INDIANA 46802

You may return this book to any agency, branch,
or bookmobile of the Allen County Public Library.

The
PACIFIC RIM REGION
Emerging Giant

Douglas A. Phillips
and
Steven C. Levi

ENSLOW PUBLISHERS, INC.

Bloy St. & Ramsey Ave. P.O. Box 38
Box 777   Aldershot
Hillside, N. J. 07205 Hants GU12 6BP
U.S.A.   U.K.

Library of Congress Cataloging-in-Publication Data

Phillips, Douglas A.
    The Pacific Rim region.

    Bibliography: p.
    Includes index.
    1. Pacific Area--Economic conditions. I. Levi,
Steven C. II. Title.
HC681.P48   1988   330.99   88-3876
ISBN 0-89490-191-5

Printed in the United States of America

10 9 8 7 6 5 4 3 2 1

Illustration Credits
The Anchorage Museum of History and Art, p. 19; Douglas
A. Phillips, pp. 23, 32, 35, 43, 51, 55, 59, 77, 83, 101,
103, 105, 107, 115, 124, 129, 132, 134, 138, 140; the
Port of Seattle, p. 54; National Archives number 80-G-
332701, p. 63; Steven C. Levi, pp. 65, 94; U.S. Air Force
Photo, pp. 75, 112; U.S. Navy Photo, p. 127.

To my parents, grandparents, Marlene, and my children—
thank you for your sacrifices, patience, and for believing in
me.

—D.P.

To Larry, Mark, Annette, and Adam Levi—remember that
those who read, lead.

—S.L.

ACKNOWLEDGMENTS

Thanks go to Marlene Phillips for reviewing this manuscript and helping me to have time to write. I want to also express my gratitude to Charles "Fritz" Gritzner and Rebecca Bowers Sipe for their assistance and for encouraging me to write.

—D.P.

Special thanks to my parents who provided me with the greatest gift a parent can give: to be there when they were needed.

—S.L.

Contents

Foreword

Sitting around the conference table in the American Embassy in Tokyo in 1985, a group of educators listened to the words of Ambassador Mike Mansfield. He spoke of the next century as the "Century of the Pacific." At that time, the United States had already begun trading more with Pacific Rim countries than with countries in Europe.

That trend will only intensify in the years to come. Stock market activity on the Tokyo and Hong Kong Exchanges in 1987 impacted heavily on world economies. Other nations of the world are inextricably tied to the economic, political, and cultural affairs of the nations that circle the vast Pacific Ocean.

The Pacific Rim Region: Emerging Giant is the first book for young people to recognize and describe this new phenomenon. While it concentrates on the history, economics, and cultures of Pacific Rim nations and their interconnections with the United States and each other, this book reinforces the continuing global interdependence of the world. We can no longer ignore the worldwide significance of the millions of people who live and work in the Pacific basin.

Japan, Korea, Taiwan, Hong Kong, Australia, and Canada are among the newer competitors on the world's markets. At once friends and rivals of the United States and Europe, this book describes the "NICs"--newly industrialized countries-- tracing their growth and power from nineteenth-century colonies or spheres of influence to the emerging producing "giants" of today.

Atlantic nations were the world's focus in the last five centuries. Now students must reach out to learn about the Pacific Rim nations that will help to shape the destiny of our mutual world. Doug Phillips and Steven Levi have opened the door to this, the "New World" of tomorrow.

Donald H. Bragaw
Chief
    Bureau of Social Studies Education
    State Education Department
    Albany, New York
Former President
    National Council for the Social Studies

"The Pacific Basin is where I think the future of the world lies."
—Ronald Reagan,
1984

1

The Present

It is the most dynamic, yet, at the same time, the most turbulent region of the world. It contains over half the earth's population. Six of the seven largest military powers in the world share its shore. From bamboo huts to skyscrapers, grass skirts to spacesuits, and mule-drawn wagons to jumbo jets, this one region houses the most diverse cultures of the world. What is this region? It is the Pacific Rim. It is made up of nations that share the shoreline of the Pacific Ocean.

The southwest anchor of the Pacific Rim is Australia. From Australia, the Pacific Rim runs north and includes the countries of Indonesia, Singapore, Malaysia, Thailand, Cambodia, Vietnam, China, South Korea, North Korea, and the Soviet Union (also known as the Union of Soviet Socialist Republics or the USSR.) These countries and others make up what is historically known as the Far East.

On the other side of the Pacific Ocean, the southeast anchor is Chile. Moving north along the Pacific coast of South and Central America are the countries of Peru, Ecuador, Colombia, Panama, Costa Rica, Nicaragua, Honduras, El Salvador, Guatemala, and Mexico. Further north are the nations of the United States of America and Canada.

There are other countries that are situated within the Pacific basin, like New Zealand, for instance. Though it is part of the Pacific basin, it is located in the South Pacific. Other countries in the South Pacific that are considered part of the Pacific Rim are the Solomon Islands, Vanuatu, Tuvalu, Western Samoa, Tonga, Papua New Guinea, Fiji, Kiribati, and the tiny island nation of Nauru. Island nations located within the North Pacific include Japan, Taiwan, the Philippines, the Northern Mariana Islands, Brunei, the Marshall Islands, and the Federated States of Micronesia. The continent of Antarctica is also considered a Pacific Rim land, even though it is not a nation.

Perhaps the most important statement to make about this rim or arc is that it is *not* merely a collection of independent nations. It is fast becoming an interdependent economic unit as more and more nations trade more and more products. Thus, the fate of each nation depends on other nations, and decisions made in one country directly affect other countries. How did this come to pass?

There is an old saying that no one can make a pencil. This does not mean that a pencil cannot be made. It just means that it would not be practical for one person to make one. Consider what goes into a pencil. First, the wood portion of the pencil comes from a cedar tree that probably grew in Oregon. The "lead," or graphite, probably came from Sri Lanka, a nation due south of India in the Indian Ocean. The brass ring, called a factice, which holds the eraser, may have come from Chile and the eraser itself from Indonesia, a nation in the southwest Pacific.

Thus, it can be seen that it takes many men and women working in different areas of the world to make the parts of as simple a product as a pencil. The same thing is true of many other products made today. The steel for a car comes from one part of the world. The glass comes from yet another. A radio may have been made in Japan, while the tires might have been manufactured in the United States. Just as no one person makes a pencil, it is not practical for one country to make a car either.

Many countries work together to produce products. In the case of the pencil, for instance, a U.S. company would buy wood from an Oregon lumber mill. It would also buy graphite from Sri Lanka, copper and zinc from Chile to make the brass factice, and the eraser material from Indonesia. It would combine all of the elements of the pencil in a factory that would produce hundreds of thousands of pencils. These pencils, in turn, might be bought by the Oregon lumbermill, the Sri Lankan graphite merchant, the mineral workers in Chile, and the eraser manufacturers in Indonesia. Business is the economic heartbeat of the world and, in the case of the Pacific Rim, the most important linkage of the nations of the area.

Actually, the Pacific Rim is one of the most important business areas of the world today, but the use of the term "rim" is not accurate. A rim is the edge of something, like the top of a jar. More appropriately, the area might be called the Pacific basin or the Pacific region. The most common expression, however, is the Pacific Rim, which refers to the thirty-eight nations and other lands located within or on the shore of the Pacific Ocean.

Because the earth is so vast and the distances between lands are so great, people have developed methods of calculating time differences so they can communicate with one another. For instance, when it is noon in San Francisco, it is 3 P.M. in New York. But in Bangkok, Thailand, it is 2 P.M. of the *following* day because Thailand lies on the other side of the International Date Line.

11

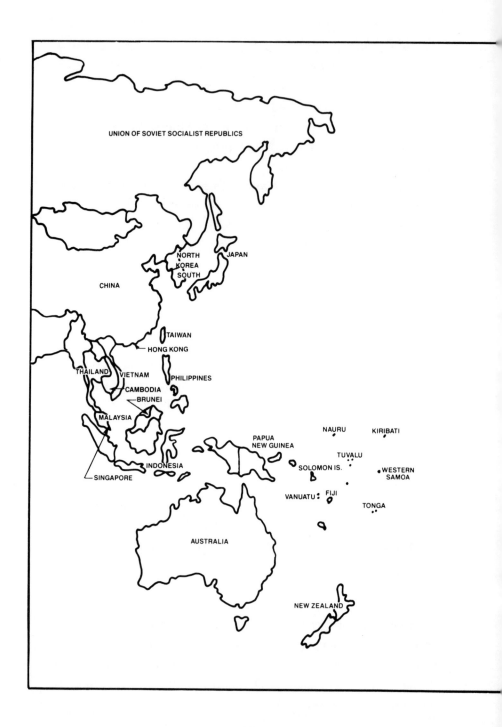

UNION OF SOVIET SOCIALIST REPUBLICS

CHINA

NORTH
KOREA
SOUTH

JAPAN

TAIWAN

HONG KONG

THAILAND

VIETNAM

PHILIPPINES

CAMBODIA

BRUNEI

MALAYSIA

INDONESIA

SINGAPORE

PAPUA
NEW GUINEA

NAURU

KIRIBATI

TUVALU

SOLOMON IS.

WESTERN
SAMOA

VANUATU

FIJI

TONGA

AUSTRALIA

NEW ZEALAND

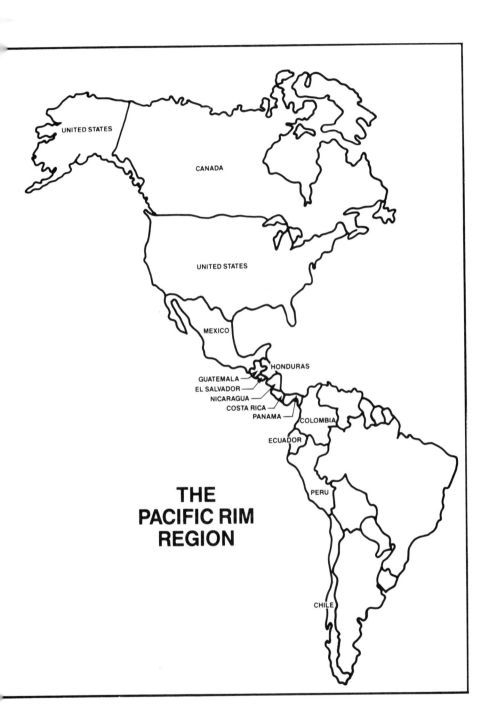

UNITED STATES

CANADA

UNITED STATES

MEXICO

HONDURAS

GUATEMALA
EL SALVADOR
NICARAGUA
COSTA RICA
PANAMA

COLOMBIA

ECUADOR

PERU

CHILE

THE PACIFIC RIM REGION

Because business must be transacted every workday, people must know what time it is in other parts of the world. International agreements have established what is known as the International Date Line, an imaginary line in the Pacific where dates change. Regions to the east are one day earlier than those to the west. For example, if it is 2 P.M. on Tuesday in Bangkok, it is noon on Monday in San Francisco. By developing this arbitrary date line, consistency in communication was established.

The date line and time zones are particularly important for the Pacific Rim because the Pacific Ocean is so large that the time varies greatly from one nation to another. Further, because there is so much commerce between nations, businesspeople in one country need to know when to call their counterparts in another country. A business caller from San Francisco, for instance, must place the call when it would be received during normal business hours by the receiver in his or her part of the world. It is also important for Pacific Rim businesspeople to know on which days of the week to call. When it is Friday in San Francisco, for instance, it is Saturday in Asia. When it is Monday in Asia, it is still Sunday in Vancouver, British Columbia. Since many businesses are not open on Saturday and Sunday, Pacific Rim business has to be conducted on the three remaining days of the week, Tuesday, Wednesday, and Thursday.

In terms of area, the Pacific Ocean covers one-third of the earth's surface. It is the largest body of water in the world. From Sydney, Australia, to Tokyo, Japan, is about 5,000 miles (8,000 km). From Tokyo to San Francisco is slightly over 5,000 miles (8,000 km). But across the broad expanse of the Pacific, the distance is greater. From Panama to Australia is almost 8,000 miles (13,000 km). Even in a jet airliner traveling at 600 miles (1,000 km) an hour, the trip from San Francisco to Tokyo will take about twelve hours. From San

14

OCEANS OF THE WORLD

NAME	AREA		AVERAGE DEPTH	
	Square Mi.	Square Km.	Feet	Meters
Pacific Ocean	64,000,000	165,760,000	13,215	4,028
Atlantic Ocean	31,815,000	82,400,000	12,880	3,926
Indian Ocean	25,300,000	65,526,700	13,002	3,963
Arctic Ocean	5,440,200	14,090,000	3,953	1,205

Francisco to Sydney it will take about fifteen hours and require a refueling stop in Honolulu. By comparison, it only takes about five hours to fly from San Francisco to New York.

Because the distances are so great, pilots have learned that the shortest distance is not necessarily a direct line between two points on a flat map. The earth, after all, is a sphere. Surprisingly, the shortest route from New York to Tokyo is not directly across the Pacific; it is by way of Anchorage, Alaska. The curvature of the earth makes a trip directly across the Pacific longer than one via Alaska.

As an experiment, take a globe, a map of the world, and a piece of string. Take the map and put one end of the string on New York. Now run the string through Los Angeles, Honolulu, and pull it tight over to Tokyo. Notice that on the flat map, this route appears to be the shortest, but a flat map may not accurately reflect distance.

Now take the globe. Place one end of the string on New York and stretch it through Los Angeles and Honolulu until it reaches Tokyo. Mark the length. Leaving the same end on New York, run the string north through Anchorage and then on to Tokyo. Notice that the distance on the globe through Anchorage is shorter than it appeared on the map? The reason is the curvature of the earth. Try the same experiment from Rio de Janeiro, Brazil, to Tokyo. Do not be surprised to learn that this type of route, called the great-circle route, makes the trip from Rio de Janeiro to Tokyo shorter through Anchorage. Visually it does not seem to be possible, but the string test proves otherwise.

Because the distance between the North American East Coast and Asia is shorter going by way of Anchorage rather than Honolulu, Anchorage has become known as the "Crossroads of the World." It is also a stopover for many flights between Asia and Europe because at the present time, most air carriers fly around Soviet air space. If in the future the Soviet Union allows international traffic to fly within its borders, Anchorage may have less air traffic.

Geology of the Pacific Region

As far as the physical geography of the Pacific Rim is concerned, geologists tell us that at one time, millions of years ago, all the world was one land mass. Then, because of plate tectonics or changes in the earth's crust, the land mass split apart into the seven continents: Europe, Asia, Africa, South America, North America, Antarctica, and Australia. Each continent was on its own "plate" and moved away from the others. This process, which took millions of years, is still occurring. Each year the continents move a fraction of an inch. If this trend continues, in millions of years all the continents could once again be part of the same land mass.

In geologic terms, there are two kinds of earth changes: gradational and cataclysmic. A gradational change is one that takes place over a long period of time. An example is the action of ocean waves on boulders at the seashore. Day by day, year by year, century by century, the ocean will beat the boulders to rocks and the rocks to stones and the stones to sand. Another eroding action is that of a river. Every spring the creeks, streams, and rivers of the world take a little dirt from the land and deposit it at sea. In the Grand Canyon, this process has been happening for so long that the Colorado River has eaten its way through hundreds of feet of the Arizona desert. Wind also contributes to the gradational erosion of the land as does weather.

A cataclysmic change is one that happens quickly. An earthquake would be a cataclysmic change. A volcanic eruption would be a cataclysmic change as well. At some point in time, the Rocky Mountains were created in a gigantic, upward thrust. Other mountain ranges have had similar births.

Geologists tell us that the cataclysmic changes are ahead of the gradational changes. Obviously, this statement is true because there is still land left above water. If gradational forces were working faster than cataclysmic forces, the oceans and rivers and weather patterns would have reduced the mountains to plains. We know that cataclysmic changes are still occurring because volcanoes are still erupting all around the Pacific basin. In America's Pacific Northwest, a violent eruption occurred at Mt. St. Helens in May of 1980. More recently, Mt. Kilauea, Hawaii, erupted, and the lava flow created new land where once there had been only sea. In fact, most of the islands in the Pacific were created by volcanic action. They are, actually, the very tops of volcanic mountains that thrust upward from the sea floor.

Many other islands are a part of what are called atolls, of which there are two types. The first kind are volcanic, the remnants of volcanoes. When a volcano erupts, it spews lava up and out, forming a dome. As more and more lava comes up out of the earth, the dome becomes larger. When the volcano stops erupting, water gradually erodes the sides of the volcano and floods the cone, the center of the volcano. Then the highest pieces of the volcanic rim still stick above water.

The second manner in which atolls form is through coral growth. To the naked eye, coral appears to be stone, but it is actually composed of exoskeletons of microscopic animals that cling to one another for survival. When millions of these small animals bind to one another, their collective hard outer shell creates a reef.

Over thousands of years, many atolls have eroded back into the sea while others have been formed. In the Pacific, there is an ongoing battle between the cataclysmic and gradational forces. Islands appear and disappear. Volcanoes erupt, erode to atolls, and disappear beneath the surface of the sea. Yet, between the eruptions and the eroding, thousands of people make their homes on these scattered islands.

It would not be accurate to say, however, that only Pacific islands were formed by volcanic action. The entire arc of the Pacific Rim is volcanic, and many of those volcanoes are still active. Geologists refer to the arc as the Ring of Fire. They estimate that 91 percent of all active volcanoes are located within the Pacific basin.

The impact of cataclysmic events on humans around the Ring of Fire has often been devastating. Thousands of persons have died in earthquakes and volcanic eruptions around the Pacific Rim. Nations in the region now take precautions to decrease the damage caused by these forces. They also provide assistance to other nations after a disaster has occurred.

The 1964 earthquake in Alaska caused violent damage and change in Anchorage and other Alaskan cities.

Cultural Diversity of the Pacific Rim

It is important to note that the Pacific Rim nations comprise more than one-half of the population of the world. The area is also unique because on its shores are nations and territories with some of the highest population densities in the world— Hong Kong, South Korea, Japan, Taiwan, Macao, and Singapore—as well as perhaps the least dense areas of the world: Canada, Australia, and Antarctica.

The Pacific Rim is also rich in its cultural diversity. In fact, the cultures are so different in the area that common behavior in one nation might be regarded as insulting in another. In Thailand, for instance, it is considered very poor manners to touch a child's head or, when seated, to allow the bottoms of your shoes or feet to be seen by others.

Food varies from country to country. Filipino foods are different from hot, spicy Chinese Sichuan cooking. The taste of Japanese sushi is very different from Mexican pinto beans or Korean kimchi. South American foods are different from Australian foods. In some countries, snakes, monkeys, squid, raw fish, or fish roe (eggs) are considered delicacies. While there are differences, it should be noted that most countries share the same staples, most notably fish, chicken, beef, rice, and wheat.

Local fruits and vegetables are usually eaten, although customs are changing with the increased use of rapid transportation from one country to another. Today, Latin American bananas, Japanese mandarin oranges, and Australian kiwi fruit can be found fresh in many markets around the world. Soda pop, candies, and sweet desserts can be seen in most countries as well, though the brands and tastes vary from nation to nation. It should also be pointed out that while each country has its own style of food, each type can usually be found in many other nations on the Pacific Rim—particularly in the United States and Canada with their large and diverse ethnic population centers.

Shelters also vary from nation to nation. In parts of the tropics, shelter is often a thatched hut with no running water and a toilet facility separate from the living quarters. In the United States, the standard is the one-family home or apartment, made of wood, stucco, or brick, with indoor plumbing, as well as hot and cold running water. In Canada and other high latitude locations, homes are insulated to withstand the freezing winter weather. In the tropics, on the other hand, homes are open to the air and built for coolness, not warmth.

Clothing styles vary from country to country as well. In the United States, Canada, Japan, and Latin America, western-style clothing is usually the accepted pattern of dress. A two- or three-piece suit with a tie is the businessman's "uniform." Within China and Vietnam, casual and business dress would be hard to tell apart as business is conducted without ties in casual cotton clothing. In Japan, the traditional clothing for women is a brightly colored kimono, and for the men a darker colored, loosely fitting kimono. Each country has developed its own style, depending not only on the weather and climate but on tradition as well.

There is one thing most Pacific Rim nations have in common: groups of aboriginal peoples. Though many of the residents of the large cities of the Pacific Rim make their living selling products or offering services, there are still a few aboriginal people living today much as they have for hundreds of years, keeping the ways of their ancestors. These people use the land to obtain food, shelter, and clothing in much the same way earlier generations did. Sometimes they wear manufactured clothing and hunt with firearms, but in other cases the changes have been minor. As an example, in Siberia and along the coast of Alaska and Canada, aboriginal people still hunt whale from the oomia, or long boat, with harpoons thrown by hand.

Some native people have become active leaders in their nation. There are also many individuals who work diligently to preserve important cultural practices and traditions while adopting new ideas and ways of life from modern civilization. This is called cultural assimilation, which means that people borrow ideas from other cultures and incorporate them into their own lives. An example of cultural assimilation would be Eskimos wearing nylon parkas instead of traditional coats of animal skin and/or gut.

There are many language differences. While much of the Pacific Rim uses English as the language of business, not all businesspeople speak English. Australians and most Canadians speak English, but the primary language of Pacific Latin America is Spanish.

In Southeast Asia, many countries not only have a national language but many dialects as well. Chinese, for instance, has two major dialects: Cantonese and Mandarin. Both have the same written style, but not the same pronunciation. Other Asian nations, Korea and Japan in particular, have a written language that is based on Chinese. In the South Pacific there are a variety of local dialects as well as French, German, Spanish, and Dutch. Since doing business often requires a written contract, proficient translators are in great demand.

Each country has its own laws. What is legal to import in one nation may be illegal to possess in another. In some countries, only certain minorities may sell some products. In other countries, laws prohibit certain items from being exported. A businessperson who sells goods to a foreign country must follow the laws of the country into which the goods will be sent.

The Pacific Rim also has a wide variety of currencies. The United States uses the dollar as its form of money. Canada

The Pacific Rim is rich in cultural diversity. These dancers come from Thailand.

also calls its currency the dollar, but the value of a Canadian dollar is different from that of an American dollar. In Mexico, the peso is the monetary unit. In other countries, the currencies used include more than five forms of dollars as well as the yen, balboa, yuan, colón, sucre, Pacific Financial Community franc, quetzal, lempira, Inti, rupiah, won, kip, ringgit, ruble, Cordoba, kina, patacá, baht, and tala. A businessperson from any country on the Pacific Rim doing business with another country not only has to take into account the time, language, and laws of the other nation, but its currency as well.

The Pacific Rim as an Economic Region

But even with these drawbacks, business among Pacific Rim partners is booming. Prior to 1970, the commercial focus of the world was around the Atlantic, but that has changed. Now the Pacific Ocean accounts for the bulk of the ocean trade in the world. As an example, the United States conducted most of its trade over the Atlantic until the early 1980s, when the Pacific became the most important economic region. Today over 60 percent of U.S. trade is in the Pacific region.

There are various factors that make business good for the Pacific Rim community. One has been the presence throughout the region of a variety of military forces that have supported stability on the seas. Traditionally, one of the greatest enemies of business is piracy, and for centuries pirates of all descriptions, flying the Jolly Roger among other flags, preyed on commercial ships. Sometimes hostages were taken and ransomed. Other times the crew was slaughtered and the cargo sold to whomever would buy the goods.

Over the centuries, however, one at a time, the navies of the world fought the pirates and drove them off the seas. As the number of pirates decreased, the number of merchant ships increased. The U.S. Navy, along with the Japanese and

Canadian navies, patrols the Pacific making sure that the shipping lanes of the ocean are safe for merchant ships. As a result, piracy exists today only in isolated instances.

Other factors which have helped make business good in the Pacific Rim include a large and growing population, access to raw materials, an expanding marketplace for products, and modernization of technology. Many countries have to import food to feed their people. Other countries may have to import raw materials to keep their factories operating at full capacity. More trade means more countries are buying and selling commodities. The modernization of technology also means that industrial plants become more efficient and thus more profitable. Another factor which has played a significant part in the upgrade of Pacific Rim economies was World War II.

At the end of World War II, many of the cities in the South Pacific and Japan had been ravaged or destroyed. Buildings were leveled and harbors bombed out. Millions of people had been killed, and thousands of acres of land were unfarmable.

To rebuild that part of the world, U.S. dollars by the millions were funneled into reconstruction projects in the Pacific Rim. The United States also opened its doors to imports from the area to encourage business development in countries destroyed by war. The plan worked well, and the flood of imports into the United States and the flow of dollars back to these countries stimulated their economies. The stationing of U.S. Army, Navy, and Air Force units in some of the Pacific Rim countries meant that U.S. dollars were spent directly in the local economy, and the troops helped to keep the peace and maintain political stability.

Economic and political stability are now making the Pacific Rim a haven for tourists. North and South American tourists travel to Japan, Hong Kong, China, and Australia.

Mexican tourists go to the United States. Indonesians go to Thailand, Japanese to Canada, and Peruvians to the Philippines.

The increased flow of money between nations as a result of international trade has brought three very important changes to the Pacific Rim. First, it has stimulated the development of local industries. Second, it has significantly raised the standard of living in most countries. Third, it has increased the involvement of nations in the region as participating members of the world community. Many people believe that the increased economic linkages will help to preserve peace in the region and in the world.

The Pacific Rim is one of the most important regions of the world. It is home for much of the world's population and houses the three largest economies in the world: the United States, Japan, and the Soviet Union. It is also a region of cultural diversity. But with the use of computers, more rapid transportation, and improved global communication, the Pacific Rim has become linked in ever increasing ways. Each nation depends on ties with other nations for economic stability at home. The economic threads of each nation combine with those of its neighbors and, when woven with other threads from around the Pacific Rim, a delicate fabric is created. All threads are critical to the durability of that fabric. The weakness of any single thread affects the entire fabric. The future of the Pacific Rim is thus in the hands of each nation.

2

The History of the Pacific Rim

It is called the Pacific Ocean, and in some parts of this giant sea the water is calm and tranquil. In other parts, however, violent storms will rise from flat seas in a matter of minutes. But when Balboa discovered the ocean in 1513, after fighting his way through the jungles of Panama, it was a calm blue sea. Balboa christened it the South Sea in the name of the King and Queen of Spain.

But Balboa was probably not the first European to see the Pacific Ocean. That honor probably goes to Marco Polo, an Italian merchant who left his home in Venice in 1271. Marco Polo and his father Niccolo were merchants in search of new products to offer on the Italian market. They spent four years traveling to China on what was then called the "Silk Road." This was the route that was used to carry Chinese goods, primarily silk, from China to the Middle East. There, Arab merchants would buy the silk and spices and sell them to European merchants who, in turn, would offer the goods for sale in Europe.

27

Marco Polo and his father were interested in opening a more direct means of doing business with China. Europe had been trading with China since the days of the Roman Empire a thousand years earlier. This trade had always been through brokers or middlemen, each of whom received a fee based on the amount of goods sold. Take, for example, a bolt of silk. The initial price covered the cost of its manufacture in China. To that was added the cost of transporting the silk from China to the Middle East. Then each Arab merchant added a commission, and the European shippers included their costs. Finally, the Venetian merchant would mark up the price of the silk one last time before putting the product on sale. All of these costs made silk very expensive for Europeans. Marco Polo's plan was to buy silk from the Chinese, transport it himself, and sell it directly to European merchants.

Marco Polo remained in China for almost twenty years. He left China in 1292 and, when he returned to Venice, wrote a book about his adventures titled *The Travels of Marco Polo*. In it, he talked of black rocks that burned (coal), paper money, and a powder, Polo said, to shoot rockets into the air. As they exploded, they sent streamers of burning color to earth. Many Europeans felt that Marco Polo had greatly exaggerated the truth and refused to believe his stories.

But European merchants were very interested in the products Marco Polo had brought back from China, particularly the spices. Refrigeration had not yet been invented, so it was extremely difficult to keep meat fresh. From the moment an animal was slaughtered, the meat began to spoil, but with spices Europeans could cover the taste and smell of the spoiled meat. Spices became so popular that there was soon a "Chinese spice rush," much like the gold rushes of later years.

European Sea Explorers

For the next two hundred years after Polo's visit, European merchants continued to trade with Arab brokers while, at the same time, searching for a sea route to the Indies. (China and Southeast Asia, the center of the spice trade, were known collectively as the Indies.) But with the invasion of the Turks, the trade route to Asia used by European merchants was cut off. This meant the Europeans had to find a new route to the spice and silk markets. European mariners began exploring the coast of Africa to see if there was a water route from the Atlantic through the vast continent to the Pacific Ocean on the other side. There was not. European sailors were not successful until 1497, when Vasco da Gama was able to sail completely around Africa. Yet da Gama's effort was almost in vain. Though he had earned a profit of twelve times the initial investment of his voyage, the trip around Africa proved to be too costly for future expeditions. Attempts were being made by other men to find cheaper routes to the Indies. Five years earlier, Christopher Columbus, a sea captain from Genoa, Italy, in the employ of Spain, had discovered America.

While Christopher Columbus has been recorded as America's discoverer, he was not the first. Native Americans had been in the so-called New World for ten thousand years. A thousand years before Columbus, Phoenicians and Vikings had probably reached the coastline of the Americas and were probably trading with the natives they discovered living there. What made the discovery by Columbus so significant, however, was that he started a "spice rush." In his attempt to reach the Indies, Columbus had sailed west. Instead of finding the Indies, he discovered America. Interestingly, since Christopher Columbus thought he had reached the Indies, he called the local natives "Indians." The name stuck. When it was discovered many years later that Columbus had not reached India but rather a new world, the term Indian was so widespread that it was too late to change the name. Europeans then began referring to America in general and the Caribbean in particular as the West Indies. China and Southeast Asia were then referred to as the East Indies.

At first, the Spanish considered North and South America nothing more than a barrier keeping them from their Asian trading destinations. They were interested in the spices of the East Indies, not in any products the new land had to offer. It was not until 1513 that Balboa saw the Pacific Ocean. Then the Spaniards realized that there was yet another major obstacle to overcome.

The Portuguese explorer who was to make the most notable contribution to the quest for spices from the East Indies was Ferdinand Magellan. Both of Magellan's parents had died when he was young, and the boy had been sent to the royal court in Portugal. There, young Magellan served as a page to the Queen, a position that enabled him to meet important people. Many were sailors, such as Christopher Columbus, and from them Magellan acquired a thirst for exploration. In August of 1519, Magellan left Spain with five ships and a crew of 250 men to sail around the world.

Magellan's voyage was not pleasant. Storms buffeted his ship in the Atlantic. When he arrived at the tip of South America, called Cape Horn, the storms were so violent that he almost abandoned his journey. (The crew of one of his ships mutinied and returned to Spain.) Then he discovered a narrow passage between the two oceans. This water passage between the continent of South America and the island known as Tierra del Fuego is now known as the Strait of Magellan. Magellan named the island Tierra del Fuego (Land of Fire) because of the numerous campfires of the natives that he saw on that island.

Once through the strait, Magellan and his men came into the calm waters of the Pacific Ocean, which he named "Mar Pacifica" or "peaceful ocean." But Magellan soon discovered that a calm sea could be as dangerous as a rough one. Once into the broad expanse of the Pacific, the crew found that the distance to the Orient was farther than they thought. As a result, their supply of food and water became depleted. With no islands in sight, Magellan's crew could not replenish their meager supply. For three months they sailed without sighting land. The men suffered horribly. What little drinking water they had turned putrid. Food became so scarce that the men were forced to eat sawdust, leather, and ship rats. Scurvy, a disease caused by a vitamin C deficiency, struck many of the men. Their gums became so swollen that they could not eat even if they could find food.

After 110 days afloat in the Pacific Ocean, Magellan spotted land. It was the Mariana Islands. Here the men took on food and water. Little more than a month later, while ashore in the Philippines, Magellan was killed by natives. His last two ships had to continue on around the world without him. Both ships finally did reach the East Indies and take on a cargo of spices. Continuing around the world toward Spain, one of the remaining ships was lost. Finally, in September of 1522, the last of Magellan's ships, the *Victoria,* landed in Seville, Spain, loaded with spices. The cost of the expedition had been high. Four of the five ships had been lost, and of the original 250 men, only 20 remained alive. Even with all the hardships, however, Magellan's voyage was very important because it proved that the world was round.

While the Spanish merchants continued to follow the idea of Magellan's route, many Spaniards wondered if there was a shorter, less expensive route to the Orient. Was there an unknown water passage from the Atlantic to the Pacific? To search for the answer to this question, they sent a number of

The ocean Magellan sailed into was very calm. He named it "Mar Pacifica."

expeditions to the New World. One of the first was in 1520 under the command of Hernando Cortés. Adventurer and gold seeker, Cortés came from a wealthy family, who felt that he should have been a lawyer. They placed him in a law school, but Hernando quickly tired of the books and left for the New World to seek adventure and fortune. One of the cleverest of the conquerers, conquistadors as they were called, he was very adept at manipulating people to achieve his own ends. Once on the coast of what is now Mexico, Cortés discovered a highly advanced civilization of Indians, known as the Aztec.

The Aztecs were not new to the North American continent, though no one knows for sure from where they came originally. Anthropologists believe that they replaced the Mayan civilization approximately three hundred years before the arrival of Cortés.

The Mayan empire, which stretched from southern Mexico to Guatemala and Honduras, started about three thousand years ago and flourished until about 900 A.D. Then it vanished. No one is sure why. Though the Mayas were primarily agricultural, they invented a system of writing and also a system of numbering, which included the zero, and developed a very accurate calendar. They also practiced human sacrifice.

The Aztecs were a highly advanced people who lived in huge cities with public buildings, athletic arenas, paved streets, aquaducts, and pyramid-shaped temples. They excelled in metalwork, pottery, and weaving. They developed a calendar that had 365 days divided into eighteen months of twenty days each. The remaining five days were known as "unlucky days." The Aztecs based their number system on twenty rather than ten. Gold, silver, and copper, along with jade and turquoise, were used as jewelry.

The Aztecs called their capital Tenochtitlán, and by the time of the arrival of Cortés, the city had a population of about seventy thousand. The Aztec empire consisted of an estimated five million people and stretched from as far south as what is today Guatemala to northern Mexico. But the empire was actually a loose federation of tribes. Transportation systems, which tend to unify a country, were built to connect distant outposts to the capital.

When the Spaniards discovered that the Aztecs had gold, they plotted to confiscate the precious metal. Gold was, after all, possibly more valuable than a shorter route to the Indies. In spite of the fact that Cortés had only about one hundred twenty men, he was able to cleverly use Indian tribes who disliked the Aztecs to increase his military power. He quickly learned that the Aztec nation was a weakly linked empire and was able to use this weakness to rule the Aztecs. The war between the Spaniards and the Aztecs was not long. The Spanish, using firearms, were soon able to subdue the Aztecs.

The arrival of Aztec gold in Spain sparked one of the first gold rushes in history. Thousands of Spaniards believed that gold was plentiful and easy to find in the New World. Many of them decided to come to the New World to seek their fortune.

In an attempt to find gold in different parts of the New World, Spanish explorers began searching north and south of the Aztec empire. In 1532, Francisco Pizarro discovered and conquered the Incas of Peru and proceeded to steal their gold. Pizarro, the son of an army officer, had worked his way up through the ranks of the Spanish army. Though he could neither read nor write, he was able to take advantage of the opportunities in the New World and became a very wealthy man. He also founded Lima as the capital of Peru.

The Inca empire stretched for 2,300 miles (3,700 km) through what is now Ecuador, Peru, Bolivia, and portions of Argentina and Chile. Though the Incas lived in one of the highest mountain ranges of the world, they were skilled farmers who terraced their fields to grow crops on steep inclines. They also used fertilizer and developed extensive irrigation systems. For livestock, they raised alpaca and llama.

The Incas constructed their buildings of blocks of granite. Some of these stones weighed as much as one hundred tons, yet they were so carefully placed together that a knife could not be inserted between them. The cities of the Incas were connected by a road system complete with rope bridges over the deep chasms of the Andes.

Eight years after Pizarro's defeat of the Incas, Coronado, in his search for the legendary Seven Cities of Gold, found no gold. Born of wealthy parents, Coronado came to the New

Terraces built by the Incas exist high in the Andes Mountains.

35

World at the age of twenty-five. Here he heard of the fabulous land of Quivera, where the legendary "Seven Cities of Cibola" were located. Bitten by the gold bug, he went in search of the cities but found only pueblos in what is now New Mexico and Arizona. Instead of finding gold, he discovered the Grand Canyon and became the first European to see the American bison, which he called "humped cattle."

To guard their newfound wealth, the Spanish established cities and forts in the Caribbean area and along the Pacific Ocean. Most of these settlements still exist today, though in a modern form. Some of these cities are Havana, Vera Cruz, Lima, Santiago, Acapulco, Monterey (both in Mexico and California), Los Angeles, Santa Barbara, and San Francisco. As the Spanish extended their influence north and south along both coasts of what is now called Latin America, their ships were able to travel farther and farther in search of new lands to conquer. However, in 1597, the Spanish learned they would have to share the Pacific Ocean with another European nation. That nation was England. While the British did not establish any colonies on the Pacific Ocean, they did plunder the Spanish settlements. Any Spanish ship with gold or other treasure aboard was considered fair game for Francis Drake and other English "sea dogs." Though it would be 200 years before the English established a colony on the Pacific coast of North America, the Spanish felt the might of the British empire half a world away.

An important change was occurring during this time period; the commercial center of the world was shifting. For centuries, the Mediterranean Sea had been the primary water link for commerce. The Atlantic was also used, but it was viewed more as an avenue to the Mediterranean than as a profitable trading route. With the discovery of the New World, however, many Europeans saw the Atlantic as the most important body of water in the world.

But the Pacific was also becoming more important to the Europeans as well. On the west coast of North and South America were the gold colonies of Spain. On the western side of the Pacific Ocean were the East Indies, the spice center of the world. Between these two coasts was a circular pattern of wind that would move the ships from one coast to the other.

There was another very important reason for the emergence of the Pacific as an increasingly important route for trade. In the Atlantic and Mediterranean, most of the best markets were already dominated by old mercantile firms. These established businesses had a firm grip on the natural resources as well. But, in the Pacific, there were no established businesses that had locked up the trade. It was an open market. New companies and established firms could compete on the same footing.

The development of the Pacific Rim was tied to both the growth of commerce and improved technology. Europeans sought new lands that produced goods that were saleable in European markets. Christopher Columbus had brought back a number of products from the New World that had sparked new industries. These included tobacco, corn, and rubber. Many of the Europeans who followed the explorers were specifically interested in natural resources that would draw a good price on the European market. As time went on, faster ships cut travel time and increased the number of trips possible during the best traveling months.

For almost two hundred years, the Spanish and English, with some participation from the Portuguese and the Dutch, controlled the eastern shores of the Pacific Ocean. It was not until the 1720s that a new nation began to explore Pacific North America. That nation was Russia. In search of furs and glory, Vitus Bering explored the sea and the strait that now bear his name. (The Bering Sea and Bering Strait divide Alaska from Siberia.) Later, other Russian explorers established cities and forts down the eastern coast of the Pacific Ocean as far south as San Francisco. The Russians remained in control of this area until the 1840s, when they decided to sell their holdings for whatever they could get. Furs were not selling well on world markets because an old product was once again catching the imagination of men and women of style: silk. For example, top hats once made of beaver pelts were now made of silk.

One of the Russian land sales was their southernmost fortress, Fort Ross. Together with the surrounding land, it was sold to a Swiss rancher in California by the name of John Sutter in 1841. (Seven years later, gold was found on Sutter's land, and this discovery sparked the California gold rush.) Thereafter, Russia gradually released its holdings in North America. Its last parcel of land, Alaska, was sold to the United States in 1867 for $7.2 million.

Throughout the early history of the Spanish, English, and Russian development of the west coasts of North and South America, the Indians were ignored or persecuted by the Europeans. North and South America were looked upon as a prize of conquest rather than a place where native Americans lived. Their rights were ignored. Many were killed or taken as slaves. The Europeans were primarily interested in the local goods and products that could be sold on European markets, not in the local natives.

But there were native peoples who were living in North and South America long before the Spanish arrived. Some anthropologists suggest that the earliest Americans came to North America from Asia over a land bridge that spanned the Bering Strait. This land bridge is believed to have existed during the last ice age. As the polar icecap expanded, the sea level was lowered, thus exposing the shallow ocean bottom to form the bridge. Though dates vary, it is assumed that people have been in North America for at least ten thousand years.

Upon arrival in what is now Alaska, these natives found that game was sparse, and they had to move often in search of food. As a result, early settlements gradually stretched southward along the coast of North America, through Central America, and then along the western coast of South America. Eventually the people moved inland, and over thousands of years North and South America became populated.

With the arrival of the Europeans on the shores of the Americas, a new era began. The Europeans were ruthless in their pursuit of gold and glory. Entire civilizations were decimated by the gun or sword. Those natives not killed by warfare found themselves victims of European diseases such as smallpox. Then the Europeans fell to fighting among themselves for the spoils of the New World.

Asian Roots on the Pacific

While the European nations were fighting each other and the native peoples for control of North and South America, China was extending its influence along the western coast of the Pacific. China, one of the oldest civilizations in the world, had been dominant in Asia for centuries because of its advanced technology and rich culture. The Chinese had gunpowder, the compass, crossbows, paper and printing, clocks, waterwheels, the abacus or bead calculator, and earthquake detection devices long before the rest of the world.

In the first century A.D., China began trading with nearby lands, including Korea and Japan. Chinese explorers went as far as the Persian Gulf, where they made contact with Arab merchants. Eventually these Arab merchants introduced Chinese products to European merchants, who took the goods back to Europe. Thus a long and very profitable period of trade began for China. The country became the trend setter of culture. Chinese art, sciences, social styles, and religion were borrowed by many other cultures in Asia. Farming techniques, weaving methods, and bronze work also found their way into other cultures.

Direct trade with Europeans blossomed in 1520, when Portuguese merchants persuaded the Chinese to allow them to establish a trading post in Beijing (Peking). In 1543, a Portuguese vessel blown off course made contact with the Japanese, and eventually the Portuguese were also allowed to set up a trading post there. Other nations were then allowed in as well. In 1639, however, the Japanese turned cool to these foreign traders because they feared that the Europeans would eventually attempt to take over Japan. To forestall any military takeover, Japan ordered all foreigners out of the country. It was not until 1854, more than two hundred years later, that the Japanese once again opened their doors to foreign traders.

Korea, another major trading partner in Asia, entered the commercial era much later. After defeating Japan in a war of independence in 1598, Korea closed its ports to all ships except those of China. For almost three hundred years Korea was known as the "Hermit Kingdom" because it refused to trade with nations other than China. It was not until 1876 that Korea opened its ports to Japan and other nations.

The history of the relationship between the East (often called the Orient) and the West (called the Occident) has often been one of conflict. European companies fought each other for the right to trade in certain countries. At the same time, China, Japan, Korea, and other countries sought to control their own ports and prevent foreign traders from dominating their people. One of the best known confrontations between East and West came about in what is known as the "Opium War."

Opium is an extremely addictive pain killer. At the end of the eighteenth century, England was heavily involved in the opium trade, and English merchants would bring it by the shipload from India and sell it to Chinese merchants to make large profits. The Chinese government was not in favor of the opium trade because the drug was turning its people into addicts.

In 1839, the Chinese government took action to enforce laws that made the trading of opium illegal. British warehouses were seized and merchants arrested and ejected from China. The British government responded by declaring war against China. The three-year war over trade issues ended with the British soundly defeating the Chinese. The victory allowed the British to continue to sell opium to the Chinese and opened more ports for trade.

The peace treaty also called for China's ceding to England the island of Hong Kong. Though Hong Kong today remains a British possession, the situation is changing. Recently China and England concluded a treaty that will return Hong Kong to China in 1997.

By the end of the nineteenth century, China was so weak that it could no longer control the foreign merchants. There were too many of them, and their nations' militaries were too strong. These countries pushed into China and began buying and selling merchandise. The Americans, British, French, Germans, and Russians took advantage of China's weakness and established "spheres of influence." Korea had been under the control of China for a number of years, but in 1894, Japan took Korea from China and began trading on the Asian mainland. In 1899, the United States was able to get all of the involved nations to agree to an "open door policy." This meant that all countries were free to sell their products in Chinese ports on equal terms with all other countries. The Chinese hated this policy, and the next year, 1900, they revolted and attempted to drive the foreigners out of China. However, a combined military force of U.S., Japanese, and European soldiers quickly put down the rebellion.

The era that began with the defeat of China in the Opium War (1842) and ended with World War II is known by the Chinese as the "Century of Humiliation." During this time, China was virtually dominated by foreign governments.

The Explorations of James Cook

Perhaps the most important historical figure in the history of the Pacific Rim was Captain James Cook. His three expeditions further defined the vast potential of the Pacific Rim.

Cook was born the son of farming parents in 1728. He left home and went to sea at an early age. By the time he joined the British Navy at twenty-seven, he had already been sailing for a number of years. His experience and seamanship were excellent, and he was promoted through the ranks quickly. From 1763 to 1767 as captain of his own ship, Cook explored the mouth of the St. Lawrence River and the shores of Newfoundland in the North Atlantic. He then sailed into the South Pacific, where he discovered—and mapped—Australia, New Zealand, and many islands. Promoted to commander, he was commissioned to discover any lands that lay at the South Pole. He never reached Antarctica, but he was the first person known to have crossed the Antarctic Circle. He continued on his journey and arrived back in England by sailing around the world far to the south of the land masses of South America and Africa.

Promoted once again, Cook commanded a ship that was sent into the Pacific to find the fabled Northwest Passage, a waterway that supposedly linked the Atlantic and the Pacific oceans. He discovered the Hawaiian Islands, which he named the Sandwich Islands after the Earl of Sandwich, then First Lord of the Admiralty. (The Earl of Sandwich gave his name to the food of the same name when he made a meal by putting a piece of meat between two pieces of bread. He invented this treat because he did not wish to leave his gambling table to eat.)

Cook then explored and mapped the coast of the American Pacific Northwest, which is now Canada and Alaska, but he never found the Northwest Passage. On his return to Hawaii, he was killed in a native uprising in 1779.

Cook's place in history is secure because he recognized the importance of the Pacific. He understood the great poten-

Hong Kong will return to the People's Republic of China in 1997.

43

tial of the lands that bounded that great body of water. His maps, which were used long after his death, helped sea traders to navigate safely the treacherous waters of the Pacific Ocean.

Cook's mapping of Australia helped in the settlement of that island continent. In 1770, Cook sailed into Botany Bay— named for the ship's botanist who discovered the unusual plants growing there—near Sydney and found what is today the primary industrial region of Australia.

Within two decades Australia would become a penal colony for English prisoners. Since English prisons were over-crowded, it was thought that sending convicts to Australia would achieve two purposes at the same time: it would get the felons out of England, and it would develop an English colony. Australia remained virtually unknown to Europeans until 1851, when gold was discovered there.

While at first the Pacific Ocean was looked upon as a bar-rier, later explorers and merchants realized that within its vastness there could be great opportunities. The larger the ocean, the more coastline there was to explore. The more coastline there was to explore, the more trade opportunities and natural resources could be found.

By the dawn of the twentieth century, much of the Pacific had been explored and mapped. Rather than seeing just iso-lated coastal enclaves, sea merchants began viewing the areas of the Pacific as pieces of a giant economic puzzle. Once as-sembled, the puzzle could reveal a complex, interlocking eco-nomic network. As time has passed, that picture of a multinational trading system has indeed come into sharp focus.

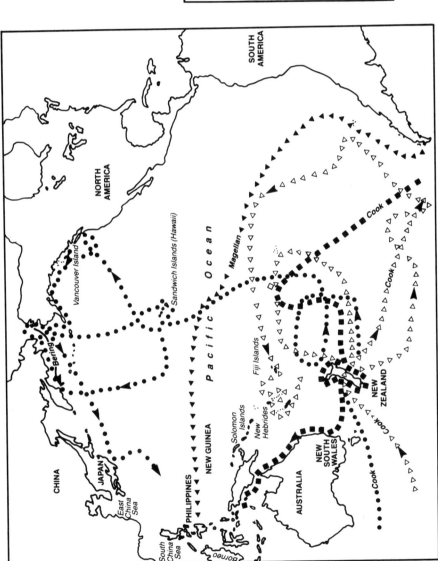

ROUTES OF
EARLY
PACIFIC
EXPLORERS

▲ Voyage of Ferdinand
   Magellan, 1519-1522

■ Voyage of James Cook,
   1768-1771

△ Voyage of James Cook,
   1772-1775

● Voyage of James Cook,
   1776-1779

> "I want the cultures of all lands to be blown about my house as freely as possible."
>
> —Mahatma Gandhi,
> June 1, 1921

3

The Pacific Rim: A Region of Diversity

How "small" has the world become? For example, consider a tourist in Asia riding down a street in Singapore in a Toyota taxicab fueled by Indonesian gasoline. The tourist could very well be wearing tennis shoes from South Korea, a shirt made in Taiwan, and jeans from the United States. This tourist might turn a corner and see a movie theater advertising the latest Hollywood movie while the radio in the taxi might be playing the newest rock 'n' roll hit. Just before the tourist enters the Chinese section of Singapore, he or she would pass the busiest McDonald's in the world. Along the road, he or she would see restaurants featuring Vietnamese, Indian, Chinese, Thai, and other ethnic foods. The tourist would also see many models of cars here: Honda, Toyota, Ford, GM, Subaru, Mercedes, and Rolls Royce.

Driving farther, the tourist would see soccer fields, tennis courts, and a fifty-meter swimming pool. Once in the harbor area, he or she would be in the second busiest port in the world, where Indonesian, Swedish, Soviet, Japanese, and Australian sailors sip Pepsi and eat Chinese noodles.

47

The diversity of the Pacific Rim is immense. The shores of the Pacific Ocean are home to people who, until the last century, had had very little contact with one another. But today, the world is shrinking in the sense that the increased speeds of travel and communication have made the most remote corners of the world accessible to modern civilization. Still, the cultures remain quite diverse. Food, clothing, religion, architecture, laws, and social customs are still sufficiently different that each nation is quite distinguishable from its neighbors.

To understand the cultural diversity of the Pacific Rim, divide the arc into four broad cultural regions: Latin America, North America and Australia, Asia, and Oceania.

Latin America

Generally speaking, Latin America includes the nations of South and Central America. The countries that border the Pacific in the Latin American region are Chile, Peru, Ecuador, Colombia, Panama, Costa Rica, Nicaragua, Honduras, El Salvador, Guatemala, and Mexico.

It is natural to think of these countries as a group because they share the influence of the old Spanish Empire in the New World. They share a common heritage as well as a common language: Spanish. While there are also many native languages throughout Latin America, most formal business along the Pacific is conducted in Spanish, though commercial business is also conducted in English. Because Spanish is the common and commercial tongue of Latin America, it is known as the *lingua franca.*

Culturally, Latin Amrica is a blending of Spanish and Indian heritage. The percentage of the population that is mestizo, or mixed Indian and European ancestry, is high, over 60 percent in some countries.

The early Spanish established their religion, Roman Catholicism, as the predominant one in Latin America. Most of the countries celebrate Christian holidays, but many local native holidays are recognized as well. In some areas of Latin America, ancient tribal customs are still practiced, even though the people themselves may view themselves as Christian.

Latin America has a wide variety of occupations. Men and women in the large cities work at jobs that are very similar to those businessmen and businesswomen work at in other parts of the world. In the rural areas, there are farmers, miners, and people who make and sell handicrafts and clothing.

When it comes to food, Latin America is known worldwide for its spicy dishes. It is important to note that the food often serves as more than just a means of providing nourishment. Peace Corps volunteers have noted that the spicy scent of Latin America food, when sweat out of the body, acts as mild mosquito repellent. Latin Americans also eat corn in the form of the tortilla and wrap their meal rather than place it between two pieces of bread.

In Latin America, the serape as clothing was once standard in many of the interior villages. A serape is a brightly colored strip of material that is worn around the shoulders or over the head. In the United States it is sometimes called a shawl. If there is a hole in the center of the serape and the head is thrust through, it is called a poncho. There are regional differences in clothing as well. In Bolivia, for example, women wear black bowler hats. In Peru, many native women wear white hats that look like top hats. However, with acculturation, a changing of a culture caused by contact with another culture, Western clothing is becoming very common in Pacific Latin America.

North America and Australia

It is natural to think of Pacific Latin American countries as similar because they were part of the Spanish Empire. In the same way, the United States of America, Canada, and Australia were once part of the British Empire. The United States declared its independence in 1776. Australia has been independent since 1901 but is still a member of the British Commonwealth. Canada became a self-governing nation in 1867 and is a member of the British Commonwealth.

Unlike Australia, which is 95 percent British, the United States and Canada have historically opened their doors to the people of the world. These two nations have a heterogeneous mix of citizens. There is no such thing as a typical citizen of the United States or Canada. While the world may view these nations as having primarily European heritage, this is not an accurate assessment of their populations. Both countries have citizens who represent almost every race, nationality, and ethnic group in the world.

Further, because there are no religious restrictions, Canada and the United States serve as homes for most religions in the world. In fact, the United States Bill of Rights specifically states that "Congress shall make no law respecting an establishment of religion." The Canadian Charter of Rights and Freedoms also states that everyone has the fundamental freedom of religion.

To the north of the forty-eight contiguous states of the United States is Canada, the world's second largest nation in terms of area. Canada is a bilingual nation. Its two official languages are English and French. While the United States primarily claims the United Kingdom as its parent country, Canada claims two parents: The United Kingdom and France. Official proclamations are written in two languages as are permits, regulations, and other legal documents.

Canada, like the United States, stretches from the Atlantic Ocean on the east to the Pacific Ocean on the west. It also borders another ocean, the Arctic Ocean, on the north. It has more coastline than any other nation on earth, a fact that may prove to be advantageous in years to come. Canada has a land mass larger than that of the United States with a population one-tenth as large. Therefore, Canada does not have a high population density, and most Canadian communities are isolated by distance. While the population is greatly scattered, the bulk of Canadians live in southern Canada near the United States border. A map of Canada will show that the major cities are in the south and on the east and west coasts.

Australia is the world's largest island and is often called the nation "down under." The term "down under" was used to describe Australia's geographical location in the early days of the British Empire. Everyone at that time knew that the

Vancouver is Canada's major port on the Pacific. It is also Canada's seventh largest city.

world was round. In describing Australia, the British naturally assumed that they were on the "top" of the globe and referred to their newly acquired colony as down under the earth. The name Australia came from the Latin term *australis,* meaning "southern." Today we realize that there is no up or down with regard to the earth. The term down under is a cultural misnomer and not a physical reality. Yet the term persists.

Australia is somewhat different from both the United States and Canada. Though the British were able to take Australia from the Aborigines, the British still had to contend with living in a very different land. Kangaroo, wallaby, dingo, Tasmanian devils, and wombats were just a few of the animals that lived only in Australia and for which there were no English words. (The term kangaroo is not the true aboriginal term for that animal. It is the Aborigine term for "there goes another one." Early settlers mixed up the expression with the name for the kangaroo. It was wrong but it stuck, much like the term down under.)

Perhaps most striking, Europeans found Australia's seasons different. Because Australia is in the Southern Hemisphere, the seasons are the reverse of those in the Northern Hemisphere. When it is winter in the United Kingdom, it is summer in Australia. In the United States and Canada, many people wish for a white Christmas. In Australia, that is out of the question; Christmas is in the middle of the summer.

The foods of the United States and Canada are very diverse because both nations have borrowed from the culinary heritage of other countries around the world. People in Canada and the United States eat quite a few hamburgers and hot dogs. The hamburger, incidentally, comes from the German city of Hamburg, and the hot dog is a U.S. version of the

German frankfurter or sausage. Other popular foods of these nations include pizza (Italy), French fries (France), sushi (Japan), tacos (Mexico), and gyros (Greece).

There are three important points to remember with regard to Canada and the United States. First, there is a constant change in the complexion of the nations because of their openness. New people bring new ideas, and new ideas bring new visions of the future. These two countries refer to themselves as the "marketplace of ideas of the world." Any idea, regardless of its absurdity, is allowed to be presented. The people believe that a good idea will be adopted into the culture, while a bad idea will fail to become popular.

Second, from an economic standpoint, Canada and the United States have free market economies and are large buyers of Pacific Rim products. They are also large exporters of raw materials. Of significance is the fact that all three countries buy the same array of products. In other words, the similarity of cultures also means a similarity of products. While not everything that sells well in the United States will sell well in Canada, much of it does. Peanut butter, for instance, sells well in the United States and Canada. It does not sell well in Chile, Hong Kong, or Indonesia. Further, since the United States and Canada have heterogeneous populations, just about any product in the world will find a group of buyers, though sometimes small. As a result, Canada and the United States are like magnets for the products of the world.

Third, because both of these two nations are open societies in the sense that they incorporate many cultures into their countries, they also incur problems. Canada is faced with political issues related to having a large French-speaking population. The United States must respect the legal rights of its minorities. The Australians must resolve issues with the Aborigines. These are examples of cultural conflicts that often occur between people in modern societies.

Pacific Asia

For many people, the Orient is a land of mystery. The important word in this sentence is "land." Many North Americans truly believe that the Orient is composed of one land and

Many U.S. goods are exported to Asia through the Port of Seattle.

culture stretching from the Bering Sea to the Indian Ocean. However, in terms of culture, nothing could be further from the truth.

The Orient, by most definitions, is composed of the Asian countries on the western coast of the Pacific Ocean. These countries include Japan, China, North Korea, South Korea, Vietnam, Cambodia, the Philippines, Indonesia, Singapore Hong Kong, Taiwan, Thailand, and Malaysia. Though the Soviet Union is geographically part of Asia, the USSR is not considered part of the Orient. More than 90 percent of the Soviet population is in the European sector of the nation.

To Westerners, food in the Orient appears quite different. While travelers to Asia from the United States accept the diversities of dress, religion, and language, they sometimes have a hard time adjusting to some of the delicacies this region offers. Some examples of these foods are snake, eel, cat, or

Buddhist monks approach a sacred temple in Thailand. Buddhism is one of the major religions found in the Asia Pacific region.

dog. Other delicacies in parts of the region include fresh snake's blood, fish eyes, and turtle.

Medicines and medical practices are also sometimes different in the Orient than in the United States and Canada. Americans, for instance, believe that drugs, operations, and physical therapy will cure most diseases. The Chinese believe that a successful medical practice is acupuncture, which is the process of putting needles into the human body at critical locations to relieve pain in other areas of the body. For instance, putting needles behind the ears, in the backs of the knees, or in the elbows might relieve pain in the abdomen. Many Westerners who have undergone acupuncture also believe that the technique is beneficial. Additionally, many natural roots, plants, minerals, and animal products are used as medicines in the Orient, and some of them are gaining popularity in North America as well.

Clothing in the Orient is also sometimes different from that of North America. The traditional Japanese form of dress is the kimono, a long robe worn with a broad sash. While many Chinese businesspeople wear the traditional Western dress, the daily clothing is sandals, a white cotton shirt, and pants or slacks. Clothing anywhere in the world, of course, differs with social, economic, and climatic conditions.

Asian languages are also different from Western languages. English and Spanish, for example, can be written phonetically. That is, a speaker can "sound out" a written word. Japanese, Chinese, and Korean written languages are pictorial. They use a symbol or picture to depict words or ideas. Since the word cannot be "sounded out," typing becomes very complicated. An average typist in the United States could write this book with as few as twenty-six letter keys, ten number keys, and twelve punctuation keys. To write this book in Chinese, a typist might need 2,000 to 3,000 keys.

Other cultural features of the Orient include the custom of bowing instead of shaking hands when meeting someone (Japan); of driving on the left-hand side of the road instead of the right (Hong Kong and Japan); and of participating in such sports as sumo wrestling (Japan), kick boxing (Thailand), Karate (Japan), and judo (Japan).

Oceania

Oceania generally refers to the thousands of islands in the central and southern Pacific. It is a vast area in terms of square miles of ocean, but very small in terms of land area. Formed by volcanoes or atolls, the islands are home to a wide variety of people in three major ethnic categories: Polynesian, Micronesian, and Melanesian. (New Zealand is also a South Pacific island but has a culture that is most similar to that of Australia. Its ethnic stock is primarily European.) Polynesians are those people who inhabit the islands of Tonga, Tahiti, Samoa, and the Hawaiian Islands. Micronesians are found in the region of the Pacific stretching from the Northern Mariana Islands to Tuvalu. Melanesians are found in the string of islands beginning in the Bismark Archipelago and extending southeast toward Fiji. Each culture has differences due to its isolation.

There are, however, many similarities among the Micronesians, Polynesians, and Melanesians. In fact, the nations of the Pacific Rim have quite a bit in common. In the age in which we live, television programs and movies from the United States can be easily seen anywhere in the world. Products from the United States such as Levi jeans, Kodak film, Pepsi Cola, and Coke can be purchased in most countries around the Pacific Rim. So can Japanese cars, Korean electronics, and Taiwanese clothing. Sports such as basketball, table tennis, soccer, tennis, and baseball are watched and played with enthusiasm throughout the Pacific Rim. Australian singers and actors like Olivia Newton John and Paul Hogan are internationally known figures. Canadian actors and singers like Donald Sutherland and Gordon Lightfoot add their unique contributions to the culture of the world. Music by American pop, rock, jazz, and country and western artists is popular throughout the world, and there are local imitators of the art form.

There is also the commonality of our ancestors. All nations have a history that often includes a rich heritage of accomplishments. Some of the structures of those ancient periods are still standing, causing us all to marvel at their complexity. The Great Wall of China, started in 300 B.C. and finished fifteen hundred years later, runs some 1500 miles (2400 km) through the northern Chinese countryside. It is so massive that it is the only human-made structure visible to the naked eye from space. There are the Aztec pyramids in Mexico and the Inca's fortress city of Machu Picchu high in the Andes, life-size terra-cotta statues of thousands of soldiers at Xian, China, and massive stone statues on Easter Island. All of these human-made creations are proof that our ancestors were very clever indeed. This commonality carries forward as well. Though the people of the Pacific Rim have white, red, yellow, black, and brown skins, they all spring from the same stock and have the same basic human needs and emotions.

Most cultures around the Pacific Rim value the family highly. Children are considered a blessing, and the family tends to stay together. It is important to note that the family often means all direct and extended relatives: parents, grandparents, aunts, uncles, nephews, nieces, in-laws, and cousins. The extended family is the building block of many native and Asian cultures. Leaving the area in which one was born and where relatives live can be unthinkable.

With few exceptions, cultures on the Pacific Rim are male-dominated. In the United States, the Soviet Union, Canada, and some other countries, this traditional role is changing by law. However, in many areas of Asia and Latin America, the thought of allowing women equal access to social and economic opportunity is as foreign as living on the moon. Each of these nations has a strict cultural role for both men and women. In Latin America, for instance, there is the term *macho,* which means "manly" or "manlike." Macho is the expected personal behavior of a man in that culture. For a woman to work as a doctor in Latin America would cause raised eyebrows because such an occupation is not part of the female role model.

Machu Picchu, the Incan fortress city, was not discovered until 1911.

While each culture has established roles for its men and women, these traditional roles may be fast disappearing in a world where nations are influenced by their neighbors. Women and men now work side by side in most occupations in the United States, China, and Canada. This development is being noted by women in other parts of the world. Highly educated women in Asia are now beginning to view college as a means to productive employment rather than as a means of simply making them better wives and mothers. Women throughout the Pacific Rim are demanding equality and working to get it. This trend could turn out to be one of the greatest social movements of the twenty-first century.

Perhaps the most important point to make about the people of the Pacific Rim is that they all have emotions, desires, and dreams regardless of their cultural backgrounds. As the world grows smaller, there will naturally be a blending of cultures and the sharing of a common future. Economic, social, and political ties between nations should draw them closer together. With cooperation among the nations of the Pacific Rim, the next century could truly be, as Theodore Roosevelt once noted, the age of the Pacific.

4

The Economic Giants:
The United States and Japan

It was September 2, 1945. The battleship *Missouri* rested in
Tokyo Bay. On the deck, officials from two powerful nations
grimly faced each other. One group represented the world's
only nuclear power—the United States—a major victor in
World War II. The second group represented the vanquished
nation of Japan—a nation dying from the effects of the war.
Two of its major cities, Hiroshima and Nagasaki, had been
totally destroyed by the world's first nuclear bombs. With the
signed peace treaty in General Douglas MacArthur's hand,
World War II in the Pacific ended.

Forty years later, these two nations once again face each
other. This time, however, it is a confrontation of dollars and
yen, not of bombs and bullets. Today, the United States is the
world's economic leader, but this position is now at risk. At
one time, an American car was a symbol of the highest quality
product in the world. The term "made in Japan" once meant
a poor quality product, mass produced, with cheap labor.
Now the tables have turned. Japan leads the world in ship-
building, steel production, and car manufacturing. It is a

leader in the high tech industries of electronics and microchip production. Japan is also gaining dominance in the world of international finance. At the same time, the United States has a staggering national debt. It has also become the largest debtor nation in the world, depending on industrial plants that are often inefficient and out of date. What happened?

The Aftermath of World War II

At the end of World War II, the United States was the strongest nation on earth. While the war had cost the United States about two hundred ninety-two thousand lives, the nation had suffered very little damage at home. The Japanese had bombed Pearl Harbor, invaded Alaska, shelled a dock in California, and dropped a few ineffective firebombs by balloons in the far west. Basically, the soil of the United States was untouched. During the war, U.S. industries were operating at peak capacity to keep up with the demand for steel, guns, tanks, medical supplies, ships, and planes. After the war, the factories stopped producing guns and bombs and started producing steel for bridges, cars, household goods, and washing machines. The world's greatest military power became the world's greatest industrial power.

For Japan, the road to economic recovery was not easy. The Japanese islands had been ravaged by war. Japan's overseas colonies had been taken away by military action, and Japanese factories had been bombed out. The work force that had not been killed was scattered throughout the islands. Food, water, and clothing were in such short supply that the United States had to supply thousands of Japanese the basics of life.

To assist the Japanese, the U.S. government gave a series of development loans. Eventually these loans totaled $500 million. This money was poured directly into the Japanese economy. Factories were constructed, and the Japanese went to work. Within a decade, production had gone up 25 percent. By 1960, Japan had raised its industrial production another 25 percent. United States aid to Japan ended, and Japan began paying back its debts.

It would appear from studying the histories of the United States and Japan that the nations would someday challenge each other. Each, in its own way, is a giant in its part of the world. Each had built a strong industrial base. Each had an aggressive, ambitious population. Each followed a policy of global expansion and imperialism.

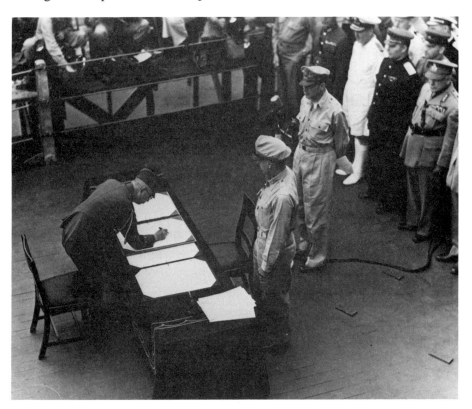

Japan surrenders to the United States on the *U.S.S. Missouri* on September 2, 1945.

At this point it is important to understand the difference between two terms: hegemony and imperialism. Both are words frequently used in the press. "Hegemony" means the establishment of a league of states with a dominant leader. In other words, ten or fifteen nations might join together and form a league of countries. If some of these nations are small, they would be led by the stronger nations in that league. But—and this the critical point—under hegemony each member has an equal vote. No member has any more, or any fewer, rights than any other member, even though one member has more influence.

As an example, take the United States. The United States was originally formed from thirteen colonies. Today there are fifty states. Each territory of the United States, when it voted to become a state, understood that it would be led by a president and Congress. More populated states, such as California, New York, Pennsylvania, Texas, and Ohio, would of course have a larger say in national politics than states with smaller populations like Alaska, Nevada, or Montana. But regardless of when a new state was admitted, the rights of new citizens were no greater or less than the citizens of the first states to join the United States.

Imperialism is different from hegemony. Imperialism is the building of an empire. One nation seizes another, or part of another, and claims it for its own. It does not allow that area to become a part of the whole; it keeps the seized area a colony. Colony means an area with natural resources that can be harvested for the benefit of another country. The original thirteen colonies of the United States were formed at the pleasure of the King of England for the benefit of English businesses. The King of England, of course, received a portion of the profits. The American colonists were not allowed equal rights with other British subjects. They had no repre-

A huge Toyota barge carries its cargo to countries on the Pacific Rim.
Japan leads the world in car manufacturing.

sentation in Parliament. Eventually during the American Revolutionary War, colonists seized power and formed their own government.

Many countries practice both hegemony and imperialism. The United States is hegemonious when it comes to the fifty states, but it remains imperialist when it comes to its territories and possessions. The United States currently controls such areas as Puerto Rico, Guam, Virgin Islands of the United States, American Samoa, Johnson Atoll, Baker Island, Howland Island, Jarvis Island, Kingman Reef, the Midway Islands, Wake Island, and the Mariana Islands. While the people of many of these areas have some of the rights of U.S. citizenship, they do not have all of these rights.

Major Events Preceding World War II

In terms of the history of Japan and the United States, both nations followed a policy of imperialism. The end of the nineteenth and the beginning of the twentieth century found both nations involved in wars. The United States was involved in the most popular war in American history, the Spanish-American War. It lasted three months and changed the United States into an imperialist nation as well as a global power with the acquisition of the Philippines.

An influential U.S. naval thinker at this time was Admiral Alfred Thayer Mahan. An advocate of sea power, Mahan wrote a book in 1890 titled *The Influence of Sea Power on History* in which he stated that control of the seas was a decisive factor in international relations. Since the United States was separated from much of the rest of the world by two oceans, it made sense to extend American sea power into these bodies of water. Mahan advocated the annexation of Hawaii as an extension of U.S. military capabilities. He also supported the construction of a canal in Central America to allow American ships to move between the Atlantic and the Pacific. Mahan greatly influenced President Theodore Roosevelt, who pressed for a Panama Canal as well as a modernization of the United States Navy.

To understand what Roosevelt accomplished as president, it is first necessary to understand the Monroe Doctrine. In 1823, President James Monroe, backed by the British, announced that the Western Hemisphere—Canada, the United States, Central and South America—was closed to colonization. The budding nations of the Western Hemisphere, therefore, would be the masters of their own destiny. They could develop as nations without having to worry about a larger country seizing their natural resources. The United States and England guaranteed their sovereignty.

But the Monroe Doctrine did *not* prohibit the United States from colonizing Central or South America. While the United States was not in a position to colonize there in 1823, in 1900 it was.

When Roosevelt announced that he was amending the Monroe Doctrine to include the "Roosevelt Corollary," South and Central American nations were upset. The Roosevelt Corollary stated that the United States would serve as an international police force. No one was sure what that meant, but it did not take long for them to find out.

When the Latin American country of Colombia refused an offer from the United States to build a canal across the Isthmus of Panama, a territory of Colombia, the United States backed a Panamanian revolution against Colombia. Supported by the U.S. Navy, the Panamanians were successful and immediately negotiated a Canal Zone treaty with the United States. Colombia was understandably upset. The rest of Central and South America wondered who would be next.

President Roosevelt was very clever. He understood that there was a limit to what the U.S. military could do. So he began a policy of "Dollar Diplomacy," the investment of U.S. dollars in a foreign country.

In Dollar Diplomacy, so many dollars are invested in an area that U.S. interests must be considered. For instance, if a U.S. copper mining company invested billions of dollars in a small Latin American country, the copper company would be an important part of that country's economy.

During the first forty years of the twentieth century, the United States gradually extended its influence in South America and across the Pacific Ocean. At the same time, Japan was extending its influence across Asia and into the Pacific. Inevitably, the United States and Japan would have to meet.

The Japanese also entered the twentieth century with a war. In this case it was the Russo-Japanese War, 1904–1905. On February 8, 1904, Japanese forces attacked Port Arthur in Manchuria. Russia, which had few ports that were ice-free year round, needed a warm-water port in order to have access to areas of the Pacific. Port Arthur served that purpose. The Japanese objected to the Russians being in Asian waters. Japan was intent on colonizing Korea and China because of its expanding population at home, where more food and raw materials were needed. At first the Russians claimed that they were only interested in a warm-water port. Later the Japanese learned that the Russians were extending their railway system into Manchuria. It was obvious that the Russians were interested in colonizing the same areas Japan wanted. The Japanese struck.

Like the Spanish-American War, the Russo-Japanese War was over quickly, in little more than a year after it had started. The Japanese were victorious primarily because their supply bases were so close to the war zone. Russia, on the other hand, had to supply troops from half a world away. Normally supplies would go across the Mediterranean Sea and through the Suez Canal to Asia, but the British controlled the Suez Canal and were pro-Japanese. Therefore, Russian ships had to go all the way around Africa to reach the war zone. In the end, the Russian Navy, weary from the long trip around Africa, was defeated by Japan in the strait separating Korea from Japan.

In the Treaty of Portsmouth of 1905, arranged by President Theodore Roosevelt, the Russians were forced to give up their warm-water access to the Pacific Ocean and all of Manchuria. Thus Russia was basically removed from having any power in the Pacific. The treaty earned President Roosevelt a Nobel Prize for peace in 1906. It also left the door wide open to Japanese expansion in Asia.

Two forces now began to drive the Japanese into confrontation with the United States. First, the Japanese began to take huge tracts of land in Asia. In 1910, they seized Korea, and as they extended their influence further, their activities came into conflict with U.S. interests in the region. Since the acquisition of the Philippines, the United States was also looking at increasing its influence in the Pacific.

A second force driving the Japanese was a growing anti-American feeling. While the Japanese had been victorious in the Russo-Japanese War, they did not feel that they had received everything they deserved in the Treaty of Portsmouth. They blamed Roosevelt, and the United States did little to set the record straight.

In fact, U.S. policies set the two nations further apart, and there was strong anti-Japanese feeling in the United States. Calling Orientals the "Yellow Peril," Americans believed that Orientals in general and the Japanese in particular were intent upon conquering the world. Numerous anti-Oriental laws were passed in California, where many Japanese lived. These laws made it difficult for the Japanese to work, own land, or become citizens of the United States, further heightening anti-American feelings in Japan.

In the Pacific, the Japanese found that the United States was attempting to stop its advances. Roosevelt sent a U.S. fleet on a trip around the world. One of the stops was in Japan. This show of naval strength was in line with Roosevelt's belief that America should "walk softly but carry a big stick."

However, in reality, all this trip did was move four battleships around the world. The United States did not establish any permanent military bases in the Asia-Pacific area. As a result, the Japanese had a free hand to expand into Southeast Asia. The United States did sign a treaty with Japan in 1908, the Root-Takahira Agreement, but it was very weak. According to its terms, the United States recognized Japanese interests in Manchuria and received a pledge that Japan would seek no further expansion.

With the start of World War I, Japan saw an opportunity to acquire new colonies. The Germans withdrew their fleet from Asia and moved it to South America. The Japanese then took advantage of this weakness and seized some German-held territory. The Japanese continued to take more land throughout the war.

The United States also participated in the First World War, but in Europe, not Asia. At the end of the First World War, both Japan and the United States had become world powers on land and at sea. Both nations had large navies and large standing armies. Japan's power, however, was concentrated in the Pacific, while American power was spread over Europe and the Pacific.

For both Japan and the United States, the 1920s were very productive. It was a time of prosperity, but it was not to last long. By 1929, both countries slipped into a worldwide depression. Japan, which depended heavily upon foreign imports, saw trade drop 50 percent by 1931. High tariffs on Japanese products decreased demand for Japanese silk, rice, and textiles. This reduced demand caused high unemployment and strikes in Japan.

The United States was having similar problems. One out of every four Americans was unemployed. The stock market, the heartbeat of America's formerly booming economy, was in a deep slump. Stockholders had lost billions of dollars in the great crash of 1929. Farmers were losing their land because of low farm prices.

When President Herbert Hoover seemed incapable of handling the crisis, he was defeated in the 1932 election by Franklin D. Roosevelt, a distant cousin of Theodore Roosevelt. Roosevelt initiated a plan known as the "New Deal," whereby the government would take an active part in helping the economy and people to recover. Billions of dollars were pumped into the U.S. economy to hire Americans to do government jobs. The workers who earned this money spent it, thereby stimulating other businesses to produce goods. In this way, the nation slowly and painfully started to pull its way out of the depression.

The Japanese pulled their country out of the depression in a different way. When the government seemed unable to handle the crisis, the Japanese military took over. After a successful takeover of Manchuria—considered by many historians to be the first act of World War II—the Japanese military set up a tightly controlled government there. This action put Japan on the road to recovery by providing new sources of raw materials. As the Japanese made manufactured products from these materials, the people earned money that could be spent in Japan. The Japanese military leaders also concluded an alliance with Adolf Hitler's Germany.

When the Japanese extended further and further into the South Pacific to seize more territory for resources, they met little resistance. The United States and the other European nations were more concerned with the economic crises they found at home. With a free hand, Japan attacked China in 1937. There was some protest from the League of Nations, the forerunner of the United Nations, but that was all. No one tried to stop the Japanese. (The only European nation that recognized Japanese land gains in Asia were the Germans under Adolf Hitler.)

When World War II broke out in Europe, Japan joined on the side of the Germans and at the same time continued to expand into Southeast Asia. It was not until 1941 that Japan came face to face with the United States.

Japan and the United States During World War II

On December 7, 1941, Japanese forces pulled a surprise attack on Pearl Harbor, Hawaii, and Manila in the Philippines. The United States was unprepared for war in the Pacific, and Japan took full advantage of this weakness. During the first years of the war, Japan took Guam, Malaya, the Philippines, Wake Island, Hong Kong, Singapore, Burma, and controlled hundreds of thousands of square miles of ocean in the South Pacific. Japan even took 1,000 miles (1,600 km) of the Aleutian Islands of Alaska.

The United States placed the war in the European theater as the first priority because of the huge threat posed by Hitler's Germany. It was not until mid-1942 that the United States was able to also focus its military power on the Pacific. In May and June of 1942, two great sea battles of World War II took place. In the Battle of the Coral Sea, May 4 to 8, the U.S. fleet sank or damaged three Japanese aircraft carriers and stopped the southern advance of Japan. It was the first naval battle in world history where the ships of the opposing forces never saw one another; it was a battle of airplanes from the decks of aircraft carriers.

The Battle of Midway, June 3 to June 6, 1942, was the turning point of the war in the Pacific. U.S. war planes devastated the Japanese fleet. In this battle, the Japanese lost four aircraft carriers and nearly three hundred planes. From this point, the United States was on the offensive.

Island by island the United States regained a foothold in the South Pacific and gradually drove the Japanese back toward their homeland. Early in 1945, the United States took Okinawa in a bloody battle. Then from airfields on this island, the U.S. Air Force began dropping tons and tons of incendiary bombs on Japan. Japanese cities were turned into blocks of burning buildings. Because the Japanese continued to show strong resistance, President Truman decided to use the "ultimate weapon," the atomic bomb.

On August 6, 1945, the *Enola Gay,* a B-29 bomber, dropped an atomic bomb on Hiroshima, Japan. This one bomb, with a force of 20,000 tons of TNT, killed 80,000 people instantly and injured more than 100,000. Three days later, a second bomb was dropped on Nagasaki. Another 40,000 people died. It was clear to the Japanese that they should save what they had left. Six days later, they surrendered.

After World War II
With the end of World War II, Japan and the United States suddenly found themselves closely tied. The United States and the Soviet Union were the only superpowers in the world. Very quickly these two giants found themselves at odds with each other. The Soviets did not trust the Americans, and the United States did not trust the USSR. As Soviet troops

moved into eastern Europe, initiating the start of the Cold War, the United States began to develop allies who would help stop the Soviet advances. In the Pacific region, Japan was in a key location to provide America with military bases. Therefore, beginning in 1945, Japan became an important partner with the United States in the defense against the Soviet Union.

Since the end of World War II, Japan has gone through a major economic revival. Its economy was dead in 1945. Today it is the envy of the world. How did this miracle occur?

There are five basic reasons. The first is the very foundation of Japanese society: group identity. Since the Japanese do not have a concept of the individual in the same sense that Westerners do, getting the Japanese to act as a group for the common good is not difficult. For a Japanese worker to do well for the good of the group is standard.

Too many North Americans, on the other hand, believe in WIIFM (Whiff-im), i.e., the "What's in it for me" philosophy. Workers often do not have a strong loyalty to their employer. They depend on unions to represent their interests. Contracts must please union workers or they are voted down.

Non-union members, such as mid-level management, often feel that U.S. companies are so large that work becomes a dehumanizing experience. There is little room for creativity or innovation. Products are produced, and no new techniques are introduced. As some workers say, "It's like the old saying: 'If it ain't broke, don't fix it.'" The root of the problem is that individual Americans often do not feel obligated to sacrifice themselves for the good of the group.

Second, with the devastation of the Japanese homeland, almost all of the factories in Japan had to be rebuilt. As a result, U.S. dollars were pumped into reconstructing the Japanese economy in the 1950s and 1960s. The plants built were state-of-the-art and have been steadily improved by the Japanese. In the United States, many of the factories had been built in the 1920s or earlier. These plants were not upgraded. When the Japanese plants started production, they often made a superior product in a more efficient manner.

Third, under the Japanese Constitution, war was outlawed and military spending limited. Consequently, more money could be funneled into domestic programs and business. Money that might have been spent on battleships or tanks could now be spent on fishing boats, steel mills, and high tech plants.

There is a major difference between the governments of the United States and Japan. In the United States, most businesses do not like government involvement. The feeling is that the more the government meddles in business, the more problems there will be. Take regulations, for instance. Many

The ground and flight crew of the *Enola Gay* gather around the plane after the first atomic bomb is dropped on Hiroshima.

businesspersons say that there are so many government regulations that quite a bit of money has to be spent just filling out government forms and complying with regulations. This money, they claim, would be better spent in producing a saleable item. In Japan, however, the government is looked upon as an active, helpful business partner.

Fourth, some experts believe that the close economic relationship between the United States and Japan has been better for the Japanese than the Americans. Consumers in the United States buy a tremendous number of products from Japan, but the Japanese do not buy as many products from the United States. Finding an American driving a Honda automobile is not unusual. Finding a Japanese businessman driving a Chevrolet or Ford is unusual. In fact, it would be *very* unusual to see the Japanese driving an American car anywhere but in North America. With the United States buying more from Japan than Japan does from the United States, a huge trade imbalance has been created.

Fifth, and finally, the Japanese have a high regard for research and development (known as R&D) to generate new products that will make money tomorrow. While the Japanese emphasize R&D, Americans find it difficult and tend to look for short-term profit instead of long-term survival.

Over the past forty years, the Japanese economy has done well. While the United States is still the world's number one industrial power, the impact of the Japanese economy on the Pacific Rim countries is staggering. Consider the following:

Of the world's largest non-U.S. corporations, 29.4 percent are Japanese.

Eight of the ten largest banks in the world are Japanese. Japan also leads the world in loans to other nations.

Japan is the world's leader in car manufacturing.

Five of the ten largest microchip producers are Japanese.

Japan has the world's second largest GNP. The United States has the largest.

Japan is the number one producer of steel in the free world.

Japan has the highest per capita rate of newspaper readers, 575 per 1,000 people. The United States ranks eighteenth.

Candidates running for office in Japan's democratic government place their campaign posters on this centralized board.

Japan has half the population of the United States yet twice the number of hospitals and better medical care. Japan has a lower infant mortality rate than the United States, and life expectancy is higher.

These facts should not downplay the critical link between the United States and Japan. These two stable, economically strong countries are the key trading points of the Pacific Rim. They provide stability for each other and for economies on both sides of the ocean and around the world.

"Anyone with ability can jump the dragon gate."
——Chinese Proverb

(The "dragon gate" was the Chinese Civil Service exam. The quote was meant to imply, in the broadest sense, that with ability there were no barriers to advancement.)

5

Emerging Economies on the Pacific Rim

In 1986 in Vladivostok, on the Pacific coast of the USSR, Soviet Premier Mikhail Gorbachev made a statement that shook the nations of the Pacific Rim. Referring to the new interest of the Soviet Union in the Pacific, he stated that the Soviet Union was now an Asia-Pacific nation. Now there was another superpower taking an active interest in the area—a superpower that other nations of the region were suspicious of. The Soviet statement was surprising for two reasons. First, since the time of Peter the Great (1672-1725), Russia had been copying European styles in an effort to become more westernized. Gorbachev's statement appeared to be an about-face. Second, if the Soviets were declaring themselves to be an Asia-Pacific nation, did this mean that there would be an increase in Soviet trade and military activity in the Pacific region?

Gorbachev's announcement concerned many Pacific Rim countries. The Soviet Union has a history of seizing land and using it to suit its purposes. At the end of World War II, for instance, the Soviet Union assumed control of many formerly independent nations and still holds them today. These nations include Estonia, Latvia, Lithuania, Poland, and East Germany. Many nations now wonder if the Soviet Union is intent on joining the family of nations on the Pacific Rim to trade with them or to conquer them.

The Pacific Rim has many nations that are potential economic powers. These are nations possessing natural resources, positive political climates, and/or a labor force that could be used to greatly increase their gross national product (GNP) and standard of living. (The GNP is the total of all money spent on all goods and services in a year. The standard of living is the level of subsistence with regard to necessities and comforts of daily life.) While there are unquestionably two economic giants on the Pacific Rim, there are many nations who have excellent economic situations and potential. A small GNP does not necessarily mean poverty, as Singapore proves. A large population does not necessarily mean a high GNP, as China shows.

The Soviet Union

One potential Pacific economic giant is, of course, the Soviet Union. One of its advantages is its size: 8.5 million square miles (22,402,200 sq. km), more than twice as large as the United States. It has a population larger than that of the United States—two hundred eighty million—and a GNP of almost $2 trillion. Additionally, like the United States and Canada, the Soviet Union has abundant natural resources. It has vast reserves of oil, as well as rivers that produce cheap power. In fact, the USSR is the world's leader in the production of petroleum and natural gas. It has one of the two strongest militaries in the world and an educated population. And it has a vast, untapped interior that could prove to be as rich in natural resources as the United States and Canada

80

PACIFIC RIM NATIONS ON THE MOVE

NATION	POPULATION		GROSS NATIONAL PRODUCT (Billions of US Dollars)		PER CAPITA INCOME (US Dollars)	
	1970	1987(est)	1969*	mid 1980's	1969*	mid 1980's
Australia	12,522,400	16,200,000	30.4	166.2 (1983)	1,861	9,960 (1983)
Canada	21,400,000	25,900,000	78.5	335 (1985)	2,313	13,541 (1985)
China	759,600,000	1,062,000,000	80 (1966)	343 (1985)	100 (1966)	330 (1985)
Japan	103,500,000	122,200,000	168	1,233 (1984)	1,300	10,200 (1984)
Singapore	2,100,000	2,600,000	1.3 (1968)	18.4 (1984)	672 (1968)	7,270 (1984)
South Korea	32,100,000	42,100,000	8	90.6 (1986)	170 (1968)	2,180 (1986)
Taiwan	14,000,000	19,600,000	4.8	60 (1985)	373	3,142 (1983)
USSR	241,748,000	284,000,000	400 (1968)	2,062 (1985)	1,678 (1968)	7,896 (1985)
USA	207,678,247	243,800,000	931.4	4,206.1 (1986)	3,687	14,461 (1986)

* Except as noted

combined. In both the short and long term, the Soviet Union could prove to be a significant influence in the Pacific.

However, there are some stumbling blocks to the USSR becoming a Pacific Rim economic giant. First, the Soviet government has such a strong control on the economy that there is little profit incentive. A worker will get few rewards for working harder. As a consequence, worker productivity is low. Alcoholism among Soviet workers is high.

Second, to be a major Pacific Rim economic power, the Soviet Union has to introduce its products to the Pacific Rim. Unfortunately, there is a transportation problem. The bulk of the Soviet's industrial capacity is located in the European sector of the nation, thousands of miles from the Pacific Ocean. Therefore, any Soviet product must be shipped a great distance by train before it can be loaded on a ship bound for Pacific ports. This added transportation cost can make Soviet products more expensive on the world market. The quality of Soviet goods is yet another problem. Many do not compare well with those made in Western Europe, Japan, or the United States. If the Soviet Union can resolve these problems, perhaps by establishing factories on the Pacific coast and improving the quality of its goods, it can become a powerful Pacific Rim trading nation.

China

Another potential economic giant on the Pacific Rim is China, the world's most populous nation with a land area of 3,691,521 square miles (9,561,000 sq. km). For much of the past half century, China has kept itself out of the global economic flow of goods and services. Since 1980, however, China has taken an increased interest in trading and manufacturing opportunities. What makes China such an impressive potential economic giant is that its human resources are just beginning to be developed. With a staggering population—over one billion people—China has a low-cost work force that will allow it to produce goods cheaper than most other nations. (Workers in China in 1987 received less than thirty dollars a month.) China also has many natural resources in its land area, an area larger than that of the United States. Coal, iron, mercury, tin, and other minerals are available, and there is an expanding oil industry.

In agriculture, China leads the world in millet, rice, and tobacco products and is one of the top three nations of the world in the production of silk, barley, cotton, potatoes, tea, and wheat. It has more pigs than any other country and uses fish farming techniques that are being studied worldwide.

China is a nation to be watched because of its changing political and economic environment. As China moves from a state-controlled to more of a mixed economy, the profit-making activities could turn the country into a leading economic

Consumers shop for food in this free market in China.

superpower. However, the question of China's internal political stability remains an issue for potential trading partners. Though it has a population of over one billion people, it has a GNP of only $343 billion. Thus its population is four times as great as that of the United States, but its GNP is one-tenth the size. The Chinese are not spending much money, but are projected to have the world's third largest GNP by the year 2000.

As China's economy and production expand, it could become a major buyer and seller of world goods. After all, the population of the world is over five billion people, and China accounts for 20 percent of that figure. This population base represents a tremendous buying and selling potential.

Canada

In North America, Canada is another potential economic giant. The second largest nation on earth in terms of area, (3,851,809 square miles or 9,976,186 sq. km), Canada has a population of twenty-six million and a GNP of about $335 billion.

Canada is a resource-rich nation that maintains many firm links with the United States. Canada and the United States are each other's Number One trading partner and strong military allies as well.

Agriculture is the primary income source in the interior provinces of Saskatchewan and Manitoba. Nationwide, Canada's agricultural assets include wheat, barley, oats, and rye. In British Columbia and Alberta, the discovery of oil there has allowed their economies to diversify. These and other provinces have such great deposits of minerals that Canada is considered one of the top six worldwide producers of asbestos, copper, gold, iron ore, nickel, silver, platinum, zinc, and other so-called strategic minerals like cobalt and uranium. Timber is also a large industry, particularly on the west coast, and fish from Canada are finding a ready market in Asia.

With the continued expansion of Pacific Rim trade, Canada will find itself in a more advantageous position not only because of its of natural resources but also because of its location. Since the earth is curved, Vancouver, British Columbia, is closer to Tokyo or Seoul than is San Francisco or Los Angeles. Reduced transportation costs, in turn, cut overall product costs, and rail lines link the west coast Canadian ports with the larger cities of the Canadian interior, as well as with Chicago, Indianapolis, and Detroit.

Australia

Another rising economic giant is Australia. A nation-continent with an area of 2,966,150 square miles (7,682,300 sq. km), roughly equivalent to that of the United States, it has a GNP of $166 billion and a population of just over sixteen million people. Australia's population is about one-ninth of that of Japan. Its principal products are agricultural, including wool, meat, sugar, cereals, wine grapes, sheep, cattle, and dairy products. The nation is a growing economic force because it is a storehouse of many mineral resources. Unfortunately, these resources are often in remote areas, and transportation costs are high.

Australia has been expanding its industrial base over the past several decades. Today it supplies many Pacific Rim countries with machinery, iron, steel, textiles, and coal. Australia also lies in a strategically important location. In the southwestern edge of the Pacific Rim arc, it serves as a military supply base and a staging area for the United States and other nations in the South Pacific. When U.S. troops were stationed in South Vietnam, food and other military supplies were stored in Australia.

But Australia does have difficulties. It has a small population and thus a small work force. Even though Australia does have untapped mineral resources, it does not have the economic base to develop those resources as yet. Australia's distance from other Pacific Rim markets also increases the cost of its goods, and the great distance between its population centers often makes Australian goods expensive, even within the nation itself.

The Four Tigers

On a lesser scale there are four other potential economic giants: Hong Kong, Taiwan, South Korea, and Singapore. Collectively these areas—one colony (Hong Kong) and three nations—are known as the "Four Tigers" or the "Four Dragons." These manufacturing tigers are also considered to be the newly industrialized countries (NICs) of Asia. This means that they have made great strides in industrializing since the late 1960s. Each of these NICs has a grip on a portion of the Pacific Rim trade for a variety of reasons. First, each has a high-quality work force that can be hired cheaply by Western standards. Second, each of these areas has good ports. Third, they all have primarily free market economics, which means that business opportunities abound.

Hong Kong is a British crown colony to the south of China with a land area of only 398 square miles (1,031 sq. km). With a population of nearly six million, Hong Kong is a well-known manufacturing territory with a GNP of $22 billion. It is already a world leader in textiles, clothing, toys, transistor radios, watches, and electronic components. Hong Kong has a dynamic harbor that serves as the primary port for goods exported from China. It is also known as a global financial center, similar to New York and London, and is the home of the most expensive building in the world, the Hong Kong and Shanghai Bank, symbol of Hong Kong's international financial stature. Tourism is also a large part of Hong Kong's economy.

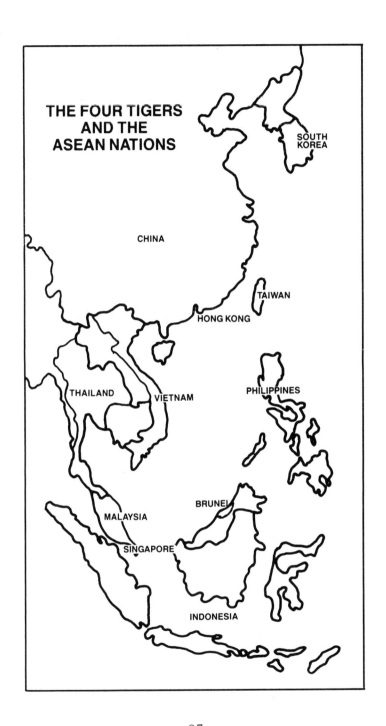

THE FOUR TIGERS
AND THE
ASEAN NATIONS

SOUTH
KOREA

CHINA

TAIWAN

HONG KONG

THAILAND

VIETNAM

PHILIPPINES

BRUNEI

MALAYSIA

SINGAPORE

INDONESIA

Hong Kong has prospered because of its policy of free trade, which means that products may enter without any kind of duty or tax. Products are often less expensive. Many worldwide companies take advantage of this unique tax-free status and conduct much of their business in Hong Kong. As a result, Hong Kong has a strong economy.

Other countries treat imports quite differently. In the United States, for example, there is an import tax on products not made within its borders. Each Japanese car coming into the United States is taxed at a certain rate. Since the consumer eventually pays this added cost, the Japanese car is more expensive in the United States market. While this tax protects small American companies just starting out in business, import taxes have a tendency to raise all prices. As the cost of Japanese cars goes up, so does the price of cars manufactured in the United States.

Hong Kong does have its challenges. In addition to Hong Kong Island, which was acquired in 1842, the British secured the New Territories from China at the end of the last century. The property was leased, not bought. In 1997, that lease will expire, and China will rule Hong Kong once again. However, a joint declaration issued by the United Kingdom and China in 1985 states that Hong Kong's unique status will remain without change for fifty years after 1997. This development has restored confidence with regard to Hong Kong's future.

Another of the Asian NICs is Taiwan (Formosa). Taiwan has a GNP of $60 billion, a population of twenty million people and a land of 13,895 square miles (35,988 sq. km). It exports textiles, clothing, electronics, chemicals, cement, and plywood.

Taiwan, an island off the coast of China larger than Maryland, is also called the Republic of China. At the close of

World War II, there were two factions in China. One was led by the Communist Mao Tse Tung and the other by Chiang Kai-shek. After a series of military defeats, Generalissimo Chiang Kai-shek was forced off the Chinese mainland onto the island of Taiwan in 1949.

For almost twenty years, the United States referred to Taiwan as "China" or the "Republic of China" while mainland China was referred to as "Red China" or the "People's Republic of China." This name confusion was resolved in 1971 when the United Nations formally invited the then-called Red Chinese to join the organization. Red China accepted, and the name China now refers to mainland China.

Today, Taiwan is economically strong because labor costs are cheaper than in many other areas of the world and the work force has a high level of productivity. Taiwan has served as a major trading partner of the United States and purchases large amounts of grain and other natural resources from the United States.

The third of the Four Tigers is South Korea, which has a GNP of $90.6 billion and a population of forty-three million. It is 38,000 square miles (98,500 sq. km) in area, which is about the same size as Indiana. Its primary exports are clothing, automobiles, textiles, processed foods, chemical fertilizers, steel, and electronic equipment. Tungsten is Korea's chief mineral, though iron, copper, graphite, limestone, coal, gold, and silver are found in lesser amounts.

There are actually two Koreas. With the defeat of the Japanese at the end of World War II, the United States and the Soviet Union agreed to split Korea at the 38th parallel. The Soviet Union would occupy the northern portion of the country, and the United States would occupy the southern portion. Before the two sectors could be united, the Cold War started.

The United States and the USSR broke off meaningful talks and conducted activities just short of a "hot" or shooting war. Then, in 1948, South Korea, also called the Republic of South Korea, held elections, further reducing the chances of bringing the two nations together.

On June 25, 1950, the North Koreans attempted to do with force what they could not do through negotiations. North Korea, also known as the Democratic People's Republic of Korea, launched a major invasion designed to defeat the South Koreans. The South Koreans were backed by United Nations forces, which included armed forces from the United States, Canada, and Australia. For the next three years United Nations and South Korean troops fought the North Korean and Chinese troops. Though the fighting ended in 1953, there is still no peace treaty between the two nations. Today, North Korea remains isolated from the Western world and has an economy much weaker than that of its southern neighbor.

Contrary to North Korea, progress in South Korea has been staggering in recent years. It has the world's seventeenth largest GNP and an annual per capita income that has risen from $160 in 1967 to over $3,000 in 1987. Democratic practices including free elections also occurred in late 1987 in response to large public demonstrations that often turned violent. In this close election, General Roh Tae Woo narrowly defeated two major opponents.

The last of the Four Tigers is also the smallest in both population and area. Singapore has a GNP of $18 billion and a population of under three million people. Only 240 square miles (622 sq. km), Singapore is an island nation with a multicultural population. Singapore has four official languages: Malay, Mandarin Chinese, Tamil, and English. It also has six religions: Islam, Christianity, Buddhism, Hinduism, Confucianism, and Taoism.

Because of its limited size, Singapore has few resources. In fact, it must obtain even its fresh water from Malaysia. But physical size has not affected its ability to become an important economic factor in the world. It is a prosperous nation linked by a causeway to Malaysia, where it obtains many natural resources. Over the years it has become, like Hong Kong, a major financial center, and there is talk that it could replace Hong Kong as a financial leader if Hong Kong stumbles. Even today, it is the world's second busiest port. It also has the tallest hotel in the world, proof of its tourism potential. Major industries in Singapore include the manufacture of steel, textiles, petrochemicals, machinery, and computer software. Ship repair and intricate interior work are other specialties of Singapore, and even Soviet ships come here for repair work.

Singapore is also a member of ASEAN, the Association of Southeast Asian Nations. This group consists of Indonesia, Malaysia, Thailand, Brunei, Singapore, and the Philippines. Organized to represent the collective interests of the region, ASEAN serves as an information and coordinating association for economic, social, cultural, and political issues in these Southeast Asian Nations. Together, the ASEAN countries are already a formidable economic and political power in the Pacific. Collectively, they are the fifth largest trading partners of the United States.

Latin America

Not to be neglected in the discussion of emerging economic giants is Latin America. Like Canada, Latin America often is overlooked because it shares the same hemisphere with the economically dominant United States. But Latin America is still an important part of the Pacific Rim picture.

The main Latin American participants in Pacific Rim trade are Chile, Peru, Colombia, Panama, and Mexico. Chile has a population of about twelve and one-half million, a GNP of about $18 billion, and a land area of 292,132 square miles (756,622 sq. km). Its principal exports are agricultural, including wheat, corn, sugar beets, vegetables, wine, and livestock. Fish, wood products, steel, and copper also account for a sizable portion of Chile's GNP.

Chile is unusual because of its long, slender shape and its governmental history. In 1970, the people of Chile elected Marxist Salvador Allende as president. He was welcomed as a reformer, which he was, but he created major problems within the economy of Chile by nationalizing several foreign-owned companies. Nationalizing means that the government in charge simply takes ownership of the property.

When Chile nationalized industries, it lost the confidence of the global business community and, in the long run, the confidence of the Chilean military. Allende was killed in a coup d'etat in September of 1973, and a military government has maintained power ever since. (A coup d'etat occurs when the leadership of a country is driven from power and replaced by another government and new leaders. Force is often used. A successful coup d'etat, as an example, might be when the president of a nation is removed from office and replaced by the general of the armed forces of that nation.)

Northwest of Chile is Peru. Peru has a population close to twenty-one million, a GNP of nearly $18 billion, and a land area of 496,222 square miles (1,285,216 sq. km). Peru's primary exports are coal, copper and other minerals, fish and fish meal, as well as petroleum. Textiles are also exported.

Tourism helps diversify the economy. Peru, like Chile, has had economic problems. In the early 1980s, Peru suffered a series of economic and social difficulties. As a result, the economy is not yet stable, but the current democratic government is working to pull the country out of debt. Peru has attempted to improve the situation by nationalizing its banks. Peruvians, naturally, are watching these developments closely to see if the nationalization improves the economy or brings about more economic problems.

North of Peru is Colombia, a nation of thirty million people with a GNP of $29 billion, and a land area that spans 455,355 square miles (1,179,369 sq. km). Colombia's principal contribution to world trade is agricultural products. Long known for its coffee, it also exports bananas, rice, meats, fuel oil, sugar, tobacco, and sorghum.

Colombia has acquired a rather damaged reputation over the past decade. Whether because of lack of power or commitment, the government of Colombia has allowed drug dealers to operate without restraint within the country. Such action has contributed to the perception in North America that Colombia is a weak, corrupt nation that encourages drug production and export. Tougher actions against drug dealers by the Colombian government, however, are beginning to dispel this perception.

Panama is a unique sea link between the nations of the Pacific Rim and Europe, Africa, and the east coasts of the United States and Canada. This Central American nation the size of Maine has an economy that benefits greatly from the canal that runs through its interior. The canal provides many jobs and one-fourth of the nation's income. Panama has a land area of 29,761 square miles (77,082 sq. km), a GNP of $4.2 billion (1984), and a population of two million three hundred thousand.

Another potential economic giant in Latin America is Mexico. Sharing a common border with the United States, Mexico has a population of eighty-two million people, a land area of 761,600 square miles (1,972,547 sq. km), and a GNP of $168 billion. Its principal agricultural products are corn, cotton, sugarcane, and fruits.

Because of its proximity to the United States and because of Mexico's different laws concerning business, many American companies find that it is in their interests to establish factories across the border in Mexico. Labor is cheaper, and environmental laws are less strict. Thus, Mexico is able to attract business from the United States. Many Mexicans near the border also work in the United States and bring home U.S. dollars, which are then spent in the Mexican economy.

Mexico attracts tourists from North America and Europe, who provide a major source of income for Mexico and a ma-

The Panama Canal is a unique sea link that connects the Atlantic and Pacific oceans.

jor market for sales of Mexican products. The country is also blessed with a large supply of petroleum. Since the oil fields are close to the United States, it is economically advantageous for U.S. companies to buy Mexican oil. The transportation costs are low because the distance to U.S. refineries is short. Thus a healthy relationship exists between the Mexican oil industry and oil-related businesses in the United States.

Mexico, however, is not without its problems. Inflation is running high—at a rate of 100 percent a year. For example, a quart of milk bought a year ago would have cost half of what it does today. Also, Mexico has a booming population. In fact, Mexico City, with its estimated fifteen million people, is the largest city on earth in terms of population and is still growing at a rapid rate. (By comparison, Mexico City is more than three times larger than Los Angeles, five times larger than Melbourne, or four times the size of Toronto.)

When we think of the Pacific Rim, an important word to be remembered is "potential." Most nations on the Pacific Rim have the potential to create a strong economy and high standard of living. Each nation has special resources that it can use to its advantage. Hong Kong has excellent tax laws and a good harbor. Canada has an advantageous geographic position and a wealth of resources. China has a vast supply of low-cost labor and many natural resources. Any nation can emerge as a giant if it intelligently takes advantage of its unique character and resources.

"We're in the same boat, brother.
We're in the same boat, brother.
And if you rock one end,
You're going to tip the other,
We're in the same boat, brother."

——African folksong

6

Trans-Pacific Ties

The economies of all the Pacific Rim nations are intertwined.
When one nation sneezes, as the old saying goes, every other
nation catches cold. The Pacific Rim, it is important to state
at this point, is not just a collection of nations. Rather, it is a
complex, intertwining, interdependent economic unit. Were
each product a strand of fiber, the combined threads would
form an intricate tapestry. Such are the relationships of the
Pacific Rim nations.

The idea of economic interdependence was clearly shown
during the week of October 19, 1987, when stock markets
around the Pacific Rim first crashed and then staged moderate
recoveries. On the 19th, the New York Stock Exchange plum-
meted over five hundred points, a loss of billions of dollars. In
response, stock markets in Japan, Canada, Australia, Hong
Kong, and Singapore had record losses. Later in the week,
the stock markets staged rallies that caused another round of
shock waves to ripple around the Pacific Rim and the world.
Because of the international economic havoc, the Hong Kong
Stock Exchange closed for an entire week. Nations all around
the world felt the effects of economic interdependence.

It is also important to note that this concept of interdependence is true of cultural and social exchange as well. The Chinese language, for instance, historically provided the roots for the Japanese and Korean languages. The Russians affected the history of what is now the west coast of the United States as far south as San Francisco. The Russian Orthodox religion is still being practiced in many parts of Alaska, and many places have Russian names. Farther south, Chinese laborers built the Union Pacific Railroad, at least as far as Promontory, Utah. After the Vietnam War, Vietnamese refugees brought their language and culture to the United States.

Today, with so many international travelers, diseases know no boundaries. Flu, AIDS, and other diseases follow in the wake of travelers. Not only do diseases "continent-hop," but so do insects and animals. The notorious killer bees were originally African. After being imported into South America for research, the bees were accidentally released, and they then established their own hives. Today they are moving north through Central America toward the United States at the rate of some three hundred miles a year. It may not be long before killer bees are as much a problem in the southern United States as they are in Central America, South America, and Africa. But even though there are problems in this interdependence, the positive possibilities are outstanding.

Improved Communication and Transportation

Business can be so profitable among Pacific Rim nations that it is said that the Pacific Ocean is shrinking in size. Take communications. Forty years ago, the fastest way to send a business order to Japan was by telegram. The telegram took twenty-four to forty-eight hours. There was some communication by phone, of course, but it was slow and cumbersome. Time zones created business difficulties. Language barriers had to be surmounted. Even after a business agreement had

98

been discussed, contracts and other paperwork still had to be sent by mail, translated, and then sent back. It took weeks, sometimes months, to conclude the transaction.

In the field of communications, the world has entered the satellite age of telecommunication. Now when someone in Toronto talks with someone in Tokyo, the voice is scientifically transformed into numbers. These numbers are then beamed to a satellite, which transmits the numbers to another satellite and then down to an earth station. All of this beaming and converting takes so little time that when you are on a phone, you do not even know that it is taking place. It happens in microseconds.

Written communication has also become faster and more efficient. As a matter of fact, transmitting messages on paper has become so common that many companies have telex numbers on their stationery. (A telex machine is a printer attached to a phone line that can reproduce communication from around the world on a typewriter twenty-four hours a day.) The telex number is quite popular with companies that do overseas business. After business hours in a foreign country, the message can be left on paper to be dealt with on the next business day. Thus, as the communication barriers drop, the rate of trade speeds up.

But there is still the problem of actually moving products from one nation to another. Suppose that a U.S. electronics store needs more Japanese computers. The store could telex the Japanese manufacturer in Tokyo and put in the order, but to fill that order, the Japanese manufacturer might have to contact a warehouse in Osaka. To replace the computers that were sold, the Japanese firm might call an Indonesian company for more plastic and a Korean company for copper wire. A call might be made to a firm in New Delhi for more cardboard or wood to make crates for the computers. The plastic from Indonesia might come by barge, but it would more likely come by plane. The Korean copper wire would also probably come by plane. Once all of the components are assembled, the Japanese computer company will turn on its power source—perhaps an American generator made in Atlanta and powered by diesel fuel supplied from an Indonesian oil field—and make more computers that can be shipped by air anywhere in the world in a few hours.

Thus transportation is obviously a critical component of Pacific Rim trade. It is not how many computers are ordered that counts; it is how many computers are delivered. A matter of concern is of course the cost of transportation. In the early days when cargo was transferred by ship, movement of goods was measured in months. At the turn of the last century, when the shipping industry changed from wind power to diesel power, the time frame dropped to weeks. In this decade, with air cargo and faster ships, it is days, sometimes even hours.

Economic, Political, and Social Ties

Because the traffic in goods back and forth across the Pacific Ocean is so profitable, the nations of the Pacific Rim have been drawn into mutually beneficial economic relationships. As a consequence, many commercial treaties have been signed among the various nations. These treaties vary, but all are aimed at keeping the flow of goods moving in and out of a country. The profitable movement of goods is, after all, the key to a stable economy.

Another strong tie among the Pacific Rim countries is the need to transfer money from one country to another and to make foreign investments. Money is a fluid commodity and can move freely from one nation to another, often with the use of a telecommunications satellite. Regardless of the nation of its origin, cash is acceptable for exchange in most nations on earth. Citizens and businesses of one nation

100

electronically deposit money in the banks of another. To complete multimillion dollar construction projects, money from a variety of investors in many different countries may be combined. The world's stock markets are open to foreign investment, and foreign stocks can be purchased in most Pacific Rim nations.

To streamline the process of doing business between countries, nations have embassies. Headed by ambassadors, they represent home countries in foreign nations. Many nations have one embassy and one or more consulates in the United States, and each represents the citizens of the home country. In turn, the United States has an embassy and one or more consulates in most other nations of the world to represent U.S. interests there.

But what exactly do these embassies and consulates do? One important function is to issue visas to persons who will be

Shipping is very important in moving goods between Pacific Rim nations. Here a Soviet ship waits to be loaded in Singapore.

101

traveling to their nation. A visa stamp is a permit placed in the passport of a traveler to allow entry into the host country.

A second function of an embassy is to assist in the making of business contracts. If a legal contract must be written between a Peruvian business, a Japanese supplier, a Canadian merchant, and a Korean air freight company, in what language should this contract be written? Although all partners in the transaction probably speak English, there is a great deal of difference between the English spoken over a steak dinner and the English written in a contract. Most smart businesspeople have lawyers draw up their contracts. Just as important as language, however, is the question, "Who, specifically, will write the contract?"

If the Peruvian businessperson was the primary party in the business deal, it is most likely that the Peruvian embassy or consulate would arrange for a Peruvian lawyer in the United States who spoke Spanish fluently to draw up the initial paperwork. The contract would be written in English by the Peruvian lawyer and then sent to the lawyers representing the other parties for their comments. A period of discussion over certain terms in the contract would occur, and then the contract would be signed. But the key point to be remembered is that the Peruvian embassy or consulate, the representative of the Peruvian government, specifically supplied the critical assistance needed to allow the business arrangement to be completed. Such is the politics of international commerce. It is also a part of the everyday responsibility of embassies and consulates around the world.

A third responsibility of embassies and consulates is to conduct the diplomatic business between their government and the host country. Official communication between governments is often transmitted through the embassy. Thus embassies and consulates provide many important services that draw the nations of the world closer together.

Today, there is so much interchange of Pacific Rim goods and services that large numbers of foreign nationals take up residence in various countries. A foreign national is someone who has the citizenship of one country but lives and works in another. A Korean executive of the Hyundai Corporation living in New York would be considered a foreign national. A Chinese student in Toronto would also be a foreign national. Often these foreign nationals bring their families with them, and their children go to local schools.

Naturally, these foreign nationals spend money in the local economy. A Canadian businessperson living in Korea will

The embassies from the Philippines (l.) and Australia in Washington, D.C., represent the citizens of their home countries.

rent an apartment, buy food, purchase a car, and pay for the children to attend school. In addition to these expenses, the Canadian businessperson will probably rent office space, buy insurance, hire Korean workers, arrange for translation services, and then buy Korean goods to be shipped to Canada. All of these activities put cash in the Korean economy.

Sometimes foreign nationals choose to become citizens of the foreign country in which they reside. The United States and Canada are famous for their open attitude toward foreigners who wish to become citizens. In fact, the United States and Canada are nations of immigrants. Everyone from the first Asian who crossed the Bering Sea on the land bridge to the last person to earn citizenship is either an immigrant or the descendant of an immigrant. Israelis, Koreans, Nicaraguans, Cambodians, Chinese, Peruvians, Filipinos, Vietnamese, British, Mexicans, Germans, Poles, Russians, and people from all nations on earth have become citizens of the United States and Canada. Many other nations around the Pacific today serve as homes for immigrants as well.

The rush to citizenship has led to benefits for the host nations. A new cultural perspective is gained. All immigrants bring with them a bit of their former world and culture. In time perhaps products that were made in an immigrant's former country but not in the United States might now be made in America. New foods, celebrations, and customs are introduced. For example, San Francisco has a Chinatown composed of many Chinese immigrants and children of immigrants. Chinese foods and celebrations like the Chinese New Year are important cultural elements for all of San Francisco.

There are also strong links among nations as the result of military alliances. The United States, for instance, has military bases situated all over the world. At each of these bases there are servicemen and servicewomen who contribute to the local economy. There are local nationals who work on the bases and bring their money back to the community. There are American bases with American personnel in South Korea, Japan, the Philippines, Australia, Taiwan, and on a variety of the Pacific islands. Each of these bases forms a strong tie between the host country and the United States.

Citizens of the United States often have a very limited understanding of the interdependence of the community of nations. Many other people live close to foreign populations most of their lives. The French, for instance, are well aware

The economies of Pacific Rim nations are closely tied together.

105

that within a short driving distance to the east everyone speaks German and uses the mark as money. To the south, everyone speaks Spanish and uses the peseta. To the north, people speak Dutch, and if one were to cross the channel to the northwest, people would be speaking English.

But if people in the United States drove twelve hours by car from most metropolitan cities, they would find that most people still spoke English, used the U.S. dollar, listened to U.S. news broadcasts, and voted in U.S. elections. The only contact most U.S. citizens have with the world of other nations is through immigrants who settle in the area. Immigration is thus just as important as an educational process for individuals as it is as an economic boost to the community.

As far as the economic and cultural influence of the United States in foreign countries is concerned, there are Dairy Queens in Thailand, McDonald's in Japan, Shakey's Pizza Parlors in Canada, and Kentucky Fried Chickens in Peru. Coke and Pepsi are in most countries around the world, and it would be hard to find a nation where U.S. cigarettes are not sold. The United States also influences the cultures of other nations through music, dance, clothing, hair styles, movies, and television. Entertainment is the second largest export of the United States today.

Another link between the nations of the Pacific Rim is an enthusiasm for sports. While each nation has its own national favorite, most sports are played throughout the region. Take American baseball, for instance. Played in vacant lots and stadiums across the United States and Canada, it is also quite popular in Japan, Korea, and Latin America. Swimming, soccer, and skiing, as well as track and field events, are engaged in throughout the Pacific Rim, and the champions from each nation meet in a variety of contests. Huge events

Films from the United States are shown in nations around the world.

like the Asian Games, Pan American Games, world championships, and the Olympics bring athletes together for international competition.

Environmental Ties

Another common bond felt throughout the Pacific Rim is a concern for the environment. All nations face the difficult problems of pollution of the air, water, and land.

Acid rain, for instance, caused by exhaust from automobiles and coal-burning industries, knows no boundary. The pollution is taken up by air currents, mixes with moisture in the clouds, and later falls to the earth when it rains. In some places in Canada, the rain is so acidic that its content approaches that of vinegar. Most of the acid rain affecting Canada comes from the United States. Alaska and northern Canada are also affected by a similar phenomenon called acid snow. It is swept northward by winds from the Soviet Union, Japan, and China.

Over a period of years, acid rain has affected hundreds of thousands of acres of forests in the Western Hemisphere. In some places in the United States and Canada, acid rain has killed all the fish in lakes and streams. Even the one-celled animals have not been able to survive. Once the lakes and rivers are dead, they lose their ability to convert carbon dioxide to oxygen. The same is true of the forests. As they are eaten away by acid rain, they too lose their ability to turn carbon dioxide into oxygen.

This is not the end of the bad news. The rain forests of the Amazon jungle in Peru and Brazil are rapidly disappearing. People are cutting down the trees for wood or for the development of agricultural lands. Year after year, thousands upon thousands of acres of rain forest are gone forever. Once again, the ability of the earth to regenerate oxygen from carbon dioxide is reduced. If this trend continues, humankind may eventually suffocate from lack of oxygen.

There are other environmental problems as well. In parts of the Pacific, there is fear that too many fish are being taken. With more and more people on earth, there is more and more demand for food. One of the traditional sources of food, particularly in Asia, is fish. For centuries, Asian nations have fished off their coastlines. Today, many of these areas have been fished out. The same thing has happened in other regions. Once one of the leading fish-producing nations in the world, Peru has seen a dramatic drop in its catch of fish because of a change in the warm ocean current called El Niño that brought heavy rains to the area in 1982 and 1983. El Niño dropped fish production by over 40 percent and the overfishing that followed left significant damage to fish stocks.

Today there are ongoing disputes between Canadian, American, Japanese, Soviet, and Korean fishermen as to who will be allowed to fish in which area. The United States, Canada, and many other nations claim as their own a 200-mile (320-km) zone from their shores, but there is too much ocean and too few ships for the waters to be adequately monitored. As a result, there is fish poaching. Indiscriminate whaling has almost wiped out some species of this mammal, the largest on earth. Hope for the whale exists, however, because international treaties have eliminated whaling for all but some indigenous peoples.

Another problem is the pollution of the ocean. For centuries the oceans have been used as garbage dumps by the nations of the world. We now know that the oceans can take only so much garbage before they begin to die. If the oceans of the world become too polluted, the fish and plant life will die. Since the oceans are the largest converters of carbon dioxide to oxygen, people will die when the oceans die.

The destruction of the environment or economic fabric anywhere results in danger elsewhere. After all, the Pacific Rim is more than a collection of nations; it is an interwoven system of political, economic, environmental, and cultural ties.

7

Issues and Conflicts of the Pacific Rim

It's two-fifteen on a bright Monday afternoon in Seoul, South Korea's capital, a city with nearly ten million people. Half an hour ago thousands of people were moving through the streets talking and chattering. Shops and restaurants were open. The sound of hundreds of cars and trucks added to the din. Then, at 2:00 P.M., a strange silence fell over the city. The streets became empty and silent. It's an air-raid drill. North Korea, the sworn enemy of South Korea, is only three minutes away by jet. Are the South Koreans overreacting? Probably not, considering there have been over seventy-seven thousand recorded North Korean violations of the 38th parallel since the Korean War ended in July of 1953. With this continuing state of hostility, the South Koreans have every reason to be cautious.

Just as there are links that hold the nations of the Pacific Rim together, there are conflicts and issues that threaten to tear them apart. People from around the Pacific Rim have every reason to be concerned. There are many problems that could divide nations or turn country against country. There

111

Two South Korean (nearest) and three U.S. Air Force jets are on patrol over the Pacific.

are global factors that, if left unchecked, could affect every nation.

Historically, not all nations have had good relations with their neighbors. The United States, for instance, has been involved in military conflicts with a variety of nations, including Mexico, Panama, Nicaragua, Honduras, El Salvador, Japan, Hawaii, and even Russia during World War I. China, on the other side of the Pacific, has been involved in military conflict with many of its neighbors, including Japan, Korea, the Soviet Union, Vietnam, Laos, and India. In fact, it would safe to say that virtually every country has been involved in a war with at least one of its neighbors.

Economic Causes of Conflict

An important thing to keep in mind when studying conflict around the Pacific Rim is that wars are usually started as the result of economic factors. For instance, Japan attacked the United States in December of 1941 because Japan needed raw materials to keep its economy and its war effort alive. Through peace treaties, the United States had encouraged

Japan to limit its intrusion into other Asian countries. This restriction worked for a while but fell apart with Japan's invasion of Manchuria and other Asian lands. As already established, Japan's primary interest was the natural resources that could be used in its factories. Japan saw the United States as a threat to these new sources, and the attack on Pearl Harbor was the result.

However, when wars are concluded, the same economic factors may still exist. Look at Japan today. It is an island nation with virtually no raw materials. Japan is just as dependent on the incoming flow of natural resources today as it was before World War II.

In terms of the root cause of war, economic factors do not go away. They have caused war in the past, and they will cause conflict in the future. Often, however, new conflicts will not necessarily involve guns, bombs, and bullets. They might be in the form of boycotts, taxes, and laws. When two nations attack each other with these weapons, it is called a "trade war."

It will occur when two nations raise tariffs, making each other's products more expensive. As an example, if the United States were in a trade war with Japan, it could raise tariffs on Japanese cars. The result would be a tax that would raise the price of each Japanese car. If the Japanese cars became too expensive, American consumers would buy American cars instead, and the Japanese car manufacturers would lose money. The Japanese government, outraged that the U.S. government was raising tariffs on its products, might raise tariffs on American goods in Japan. American companies would then lose money in Japan.

Why do nations start to raise tariffs in the first place? Tariffs are ways of showing dissatisfaction and protecting industries at home. When the United States is unhappy with a

Japanese policy, the raising of the tariff is a nonviolent way of saying that the United States does not like a particular policy. Another way of showing dissatisfaction is to cut off trade. As an example, when the Soviet Union invaded Afghanistan, President Carter stopped selling grain to the USSR. This was the President's way of saying that the United States was protesting the Soviet military actions.

Tariffs also protect industry at home by raising the cost of imported products. As a result, consumers tend to buy the more inexpensive products of their country.

Whatever the causes of a real war, people are killed and injured during the conflict. In the Vietnam War, for instance, the United States lost more than fifty-seven thousand soldiers and had more than one hundred fifty thousand other war-related injuries. As a result, over two hundred thousand families across the United States were touched directly by the war.

These bad feelings frequently do not disappear. Over the years many people who remember World War II, the Korean War, or the Vietnam War have lingering hatreds that turn up in the marketplace. There are still people today who will not buy a Japanese or German car because they had a loved one killed or injured in World War II.

Suppose that every casualty of the Vietnam War came from a home with three other people in it. The result might be that 844,000 people in the United States would not buy products from Vietnam. As these people grow up, they may convince friends not to buy products from Vietnam, and that number might increase. While this dislike of Vietnam will pass, it will take years, perhaps decades. During that time, Vietnamese products will not sell well in U.S. markets.

The refusal of a consumer anywhere in the world to buy a product is a right of the consumer. It is also an important

The United States followed the French into the long conflict in Vietnam. This memorial in Washington, D.C., serves as a reminder of that war.

grass roots form of political and economic pressure. When people spend money, they are voting with their pocketbooks. They are supporting certain products and the companies and countries that produce that product. When a boycott begins, it is the dollar diplomacy of hundreds of thousands of consumers voting together with their pocketbooks. If the Japanese government does something that upsets the people of the United States, the people may show their resentment by not buying Japanese products. When the Japanese companies lose money, they will go to the Japanese government and demand a change in national policy. While this is a short version of a long story, it does show how consumer power works.

If wars are caused by economic factors that are not solved by the war and wars cause consumers to stop buying products, what possible good do wars accomplish? Unfortunately, there is an answer.

War is expensive, very expensive. It costs nations in dollars and lives, but it is also a great stimulator of the economy. Just before World War II, the world was in the midst of a deep depression. In the United States, unemployment was high, factories were closing, farms were being repossessed, banks were going bankrupt, and the stockmarket had crashed.

To carry on the war, it was necessary for the U. S. government to "hire" men and women to serve in its armed forces. It was also necessary to contract with companies to make airplanes, guns, ships, uniforms, bombs, and other implements of war. All of the people employed earned money. When spent, this money stimulated the economy. However, if the government was broke, where did it find the money to hire these people and contract with the companies? The U. S. government solved this problem by what is called "deficit spending."

Deficit Spending

There are many ways of pulling a nation back onto its economic feet. One way is known as "deficit spending," spending more than you earn. In other words, if a nation took in $1 billion in taxes and spent $2 billion, it would have a deficit, or a debt, of $1 billion.

Deficit spending, while a bad idea for the long run, is not an unreasonable idea for the short run. In reality, for the short term, deficit spending is similar to a business making an investment. You spend money to buy raw materials. You spend money to build a factory. You spend money to hire workers. You spend money to hire a sales staff. You spend money to insure the plant. Then, finally, when you produce a product, money starts to come in the front door. But until you have a product to sell, you spend money. Such spending or borrowing is the nature of business.

For the short run, business and governments are much the same. In times of economic crisis, governments often practice deficit spending. But if the deficit spending continues for too long a period, major economic disasters may result.

When Franklin D. Roosevelt was elected president in 1932, the U.S. economy was dying. The nation was not buying goods from other countries, so those countries were having economic problems as well. FDR began resolving the economic woes in the United States by deficit spending. He allowed the U.S. government to spend money it had not earned. Where did he get the money? He borrowed it from a variety of sources but mostly from banks.

Thus, the U.S. government hired hundreds of thousands of unemployed people. People made roads, monuments, and other civic projects, and every worker earned a salary. As soon as they started earning money, these people spent that money. They made house and car payments. They bought food, clothes, lumber, and glass. This spending, in turn, stimulated the food, clothing, lumber, and glass industries, which then had money to hire more workers. These newly hired workers spent their salaries on house and car payments as well as on food, clothing, lumber, and glass. Eventually the government earned back much of the money it had borrowed through taxes.

But there is a downside to deficit spending. As it goes from short term to long term, inflation sets in. Inflation is too much money chasing a limited supply of goods. In other words, inflation is when so many people want a certain item that the price of that item goes up. For example, as thousands and thousands of people earn money, they may all want to buy cars. Yet, there may not be enough cars for everyone to buy. If the demand for cars is greater than the supply, prices will increase. If car prices and profits are high, the supply of cars will usually increase. (This is known as the law of supply and demand.) As products become more expensive for consumers, they also become more expensive for governments. The governments have to pay more for a bulldozer as the rate of inflation increases.

To offset this increase in prices, governments then borrow more money to keep up with inflation, and the inflation gets worse. This trend continues as long as the government continues to pump money into the economy. In some countries of the Pacific Rim, annual inflation rates have run over 100 percent.

The federal deficit in the United States now greatly exceeds two trillion dollars. This deficit spending, at some time, may have a chilling impact on the economy in the United States. But the impact in other Pacific Rim nations will also be staggering. Americans will buy fewer cars, stereos, and cameras, many of them Japanese. Americans may buy fewer shoes, which will put a pinch in the leather industry in Colombia. Americans will also travel less and buy fewer bananas, sweaters, computers, toys, cosmetics, and silk suits. Then the impact begins to multiply.

Because American consumers cannot afford Japanese cars, the Japanese cars have to be sold somewhere else. If the Hondas cannot be sold in the United States, they might be sold in Latin America. But because U.S. consumers have stopped buying Latin American products, there is a recession in Latin America as well. Since the Japanese cars cannot sell at full price, the Honda company might drop the price of its automobiles lower and lower until the cars are sold. In a recession, the cars might have to be sold at a loss, which translates into less money for the Honda company and adds to economic difficulties in Japan. It would also translate into a loss in the United States because so many Japanese yen—in the form of dollars—are invested in the stock market and in construction projects. If the Japanese must cut back on investment in the United States, the U.S. economy will suffer as well.

For Japan, the news also gets worse. Japan will take the brunt of the economic cutback. Not only will the Japanese car industry be hurt, but so will the Japanese computer, television, recorder, and communications industries. These companies will have a product to sell but less demand for the product.

Worse yet, throughout the Pacific Rim, other businesses in other countries will be affected by the lack of buying by consumers in the United States. Known as the multiplier effect, it means that an economic crisis gets worse as it travels farther. If any company cannot pay its bills, it does not pay its employees. The employees, in turn, cannot pay for their homes, cars, etc. This is the multiplier effect in action, and in the end the economies affected are less productive.

Another problem facing the United States, and ultimately the Pacific Rim, is that the usual steady increase of productivity in the United States is declining. At one time the United States was a powerhouse of industrial technology. Products from the United States were of fine quality and durability. But those days seem to have passed. Products from the United States today are often expensive, poorer in quality, and usable for only a limited period of time. What happened?

There are a variety of causes. First, of course, is improved foreign competition. The Japanese began producing a car cheaper than U.S. firms. In order to compete on the basis of price in the world market, the quality of U.S. cars went down. But the problems went deeper. The Japanese placed large amounts of money in research and development and produced a high-quality small car for markets in the United States. The U.S. car manufacturers did not produce a small car. They kept manufacturing the big gas guzzlers. In the early 1970s, when the oil crisis hit, U.S. consumers started buying small, fuel-efficient cars. The result was a tremendous boom for the Japanese car manufacturers and a bust for the American car manufacturers.

If this boom for the Japanese car manufacturers and bust for the American car manufacturers continues, an imbalance of trade will result. Most often called a trade deficit by the United States, this means that more money is being spent by U.S. citizens on foreign products than is being spent by foreigners on U.S. products. In economic terms, this means that the American dollar is "weak," or that it has less buying power. The American dollar will continue to remain weak as long as more money flows out of instead of back into the United States. Why? Because as more dollars flow out of the United States, there are fewer dollars to circulate inside the United States. Fewer dollars mean that interest rates go up and businesses cannot afford to borrow money. This, in turn, means fewer American products are made. In the long run, a weak dollar may mean a recession.

Is the dollar weaker today? In mid-1985, a U.S. dollar was worth 248 Japanese yen. A dollar bought 160 yen at the end of 1986. At the beginning of 1988, one dollar was worth only 125 yen.

However, there is a positive side to a weak dollar. When the American dollar is low, American products are good buys on foreign markets. An American automobile that cost $10,000 on the Japanese market one year might cost $8,000 the next year. When the American dollar falls, U.S. products become cheaper for foreign buyers. Following the law of supply and demand, there will come a point when foreigners will begin to buy American products because the quality is good and the price is low.

Another reason for lower U.S. productivity is that, in the United States, money invested is often less risky than money put into a business. People in the United States with money to invest will most likely place it in a bank to earn a modest rate of interest rather than risk it in a business venture. As a result, money that should have been invested to make quality products is sitting in a bank drawing interest.

Do these dollars going to Japan return to the United States? Yes they do, but not in the form of profit from the sale of American products. The Japanese do not buy many manufactured products from the United States, but they are buying up U.S. stocks and Treasury bonds as well as investment companies. The United States is also buying foreign stocks at a record pace. But on the balance sheet, the United States is now the world's largest debtor nation, borrowing more money than it lends. The United States must now borrow to support its own economy.

The situation gets worse. There are factors that work against the United States getting back on its economic feet. First, there is the lack of commitment to reduce the deficit of the federal government. It was easy to build, but it will be difficult to reduce. The president of the United States and the U.S. Congress constantly discuss budget matters, but they have not been able to develop a deficit-fighting plan that both agree upon.

Also, the United States is currently locked in what is referred to as the tort reform crisis. Tort reform is a term used to describe the problems that have arisen in regard to liability insurance. Under U.S. law, if a person is injured, that person has a right to recover damages. The injured party goes to court, asks for payment of a certain amount of money to cover his or her injuries, and then allows a judge and jury to settle the award. This is a reasonable way for injured people to be compensated for damage to their property and body.

With the virtual flood of insurance lawsuits in recent years, insurance companies are no longer insuring many American products. Businesses must produce a product without insurance or raise the price of the product to afford insurance. The result is that any lawsuit must be paid out-of-pocket. Across the United States, many businesses prefer to stop manufacturing certain products or to close their factories rather than run the risk of a lawsuit that could cost them millions. In the short and long term, this practice means fewer American products on the world market and a growth of the U.S. deficit.

Unfortunately, just about every country on the Pacific Rim has long-term economic challenges. The possibility of inflation is present throughout the region. Deficits are also rising in many nations. What makes the Pacific Rim so vulnerable to economic disaster is that much of the money borrowed by Pacific Rim countries comes from private banks and the World Bank. (The World Bank is an international lending institution whose customers are countries, not businesses.) But the United States controls the World Bank. If there are economic problems in the United States, everyone living in the Pacific Rim will feel the economic pinch.

Social and Political Issues Facing the Region

The stability of the Pacific Rim is also threatened by the rising population of the world. Over one-half of the world's population lives in the nations around the Pacific. Birthrates, the number of children born per one thousand people, vary from very low in Japan, the United States, and China, to some of the highest in the world in Peru, Mexico, and Vietnam. In general, birthrates are rising faster in Third World countries than in the First and Second World countries.

At the end of World War II and the beginning of the Cold War, the world was divided into three factions. Those nations allied with the United States are known as First World countries. Those nations allied with the Soviet Union—usually referred to as communist bloc countries—are called Second World nations. The balance of the world is known as Third World or nonaligned countries.

Unfortunately, the term Third World sometimes has a negative image. Often a Third World nation is considered a backward nation. While there are some Third World nations that fit this assessment, most do not. Some Third World countries like Saudi Arabia and Kuwait have very high standards of living.

In the long run, with the possible exception of China and the Soviet Union, a declining birthrate could mean less productivity in the First and Second worlds and more consumption in the Third World. If there were lower population

The Soviet Embassy in Washington, D.C., helps to connect the nations of the First World with those nations of the Second World.

increases in the United States and substantial population increases in Latin America, then eventually a massive migration from Latin America to the First and Second world countries might occur. This move would further change the face of the globe.

Another issue facing the Pacific Rim is discrimination. Prejudice against minorities, the elderly, or women is unfortunate in any society, but it remains an issue of conflict in parts of the region.

As an example, take racism. The most obvious difficulty with racism is that it is a blind hatred that has no basis in fact. Usually the dislike is summed up in supposed national character traits or stereotypes. To label an entire race, however, is untrue and racist.

While racism is a poor practice to follow personally, it is economic suicide for business. There, decisions must be made for the good of the business, not for any individual. What links the Pacific Rim nations in an economic unit is each country's need for the goods and products of every other country. Racism threatens to tear this fabric apart. Frequently, aboriginal groups and recent immigrants become the targets of racist attacks.

Although many laws have helped to lessen the impact of racism, sexism, age-ism, and other forms of discrimination existing around the Pacific Rim, the problems still exist in many societies.

There are other issues as well. The cry for more power to be left in the hands of the voting public is being heard around the Pacific Rim. A decade ago, it was believed by many nations that a strong central government controlled by the military was necessary for the stability of the nation, but times have changed. Tired of control by the military, nation after nation has opted for or fought to release more and more power to the people. When elected officials fail to meet the commitments made to the voters, often they are ousted by a vote of the people. In the Philippines, the demand for the removal of Ferdinand Marcos was followed by the installation of Corazon Aquino as president. In South Korea, massive demonstrations by the people forced the acceleration of democratic practices and relatively free elections for president in 1987. In China, students have protested in favor of democracy, and even in the Soviet Union, more than one name is now appearing on ballots for some offices. The demand for democracy is spreading throughout the region, and more democratic governments are appearing on both coasts of the Pacific Ocean.

Military Tension in the Region

The most unsettling question regarding the Pacific Rim is its potential for war. The region is the most militarized area of the world. The United States and the Soviet Union have the largest navies in the world and look at the Pacific Ocean as a military buffer area that separates one nation from the other. The persistent distrust of each other gives rise to a continued Cold War. This is a holdover from the period after World War II when the Western powers and the Soviet Union were engaged in a political and economic struggle and any form of meaningful discussion virtually ceased. This era produced a feeling of deep mutual distrust that has been felt by nations around the world.

For the Soviet Union, the Cold War bred a feeling of mistrust for the United States and its allies. The Soviet Union believed that the United States was intent on subverting the Soviet system with spies and economic sabotage. The United

Soviet and U.S. militaries often "test" each other in the Pacific region.

States feared that the Soviet brand of socialism was spreading too fast and too far. Soviet influence was appearing throughout Latin America, Europe, and Asia. The United States believed that Soviet Marxism and expansionist policies had to be met and stopped at every location in the world.

To this end, the United States formed a number of looseknit military defense networks. One, on the Pacific Rim, formed in 1954, was known as SEATO, the Southeast Asia Treaty Organization. SEATO was designed so that if any member of the organization was attacked by the Soviet Union, every other nation in the organization would come to its aid. This was an admirable idea, but it had two flaws. First, the Soviet Union did not invade with its armies; when it did apply pressure, it was indirect or covert, making a military commitment hard to implement. In other words, if the Soviet Union backed guerillas fighting in Vietnam would such action require other SEATO members to go to war in Vietnam? Some members did not. The subsequent bickering among SEATO powers led to a weakening of the organization and its ultimate death in 1977.

A second flaw is that the concept of SEATO and other defense alliances added credibility to the idea that there was an active conflict between the United States and the Soviet Union and strengthened the belief that the Soviet Union was bent on world domination. Thus, to SEATO members, anything the Soviet Union did or proposed was based on long-term domination of the world. The impact of this mentality still pervades areas of the Pacific Rim. Many businesspeople are reluctant to trade with the Soviet Union because they believe that any dealings could open the door to potential domination of the world by the Soviets.

However, it is important to understand that even though SEATO is no longer a peacekeeping alliance, the Pacific Rim is still a military powder keg. Six of the seven largest standing armies exist there: the Soviet Union, China, the United States, Vietnam, South Korea, and North Korea. These nations are generally divided into two camps, each with roots in the Cold War. Conflict between these two camps has occurred within the last three decades in China, Vietnam, and Korea.

The long-term impact of the Cold War mentality is staggering. Even though many nations disagree with the policies of the Soviet Union, the USSR is still a member of the community of nations. The Soviet Union has a powerful impact upon the Pacific Rim, and the nation may eventually become an economic leader in the region. But until that time, many Pacific Rim nations will continue to treat the Soviet Union as an unsavory economic partner and a dangerous ally. As an example of this Cold War, South Korea has very little official trade with North Korea, even though the 38th parallel dividing the former nation is barely beyond the city limits of Seoul.

Cold War mentality also continues to be a part of the conflict existing between China and Taiwan. Forced to retreat to the island of Taiwan after the communist takeover in 1949,

An honor guard in Taiwan reminds visitors of Taiwan's continuing conflict with China.

the Nationalists established the Republic of China, which remains bitterly opposed to the mainland nation called the People's Republic of China.

Other economic, political, and social tensions still exist in the region. Millions of Chinese and Soviet soldiers face each other with distrust across their long common border. Vietnam remains at odds with China, Cambodia, and Thailand. Civil strife also exists in a number of nations. The Philippines, Fiji, Thailand, Cambodia, Nicaragua, and Peru all face armed threats from within their own borders.

While the Pacific Rim does have strong ties between its countries, there are also economic, social, and political forces that threaten to tear the region apart. There is no guarantee that the nations will continue to interact with one another in peace and harmony. But there is hope that the reasons for working cooperatively are more numerous than those threatening to destroy the Pacific Rim.

"It is my conviction that a great Pacific age will soon unfold as the result of continuing cooperation among . . . Pacific basin countries in the political, economic, cultural, and other fields."

—Chun Doo Hwan,
1981

8

The Future of the Pacific Rim

There is an old vaudeville adage that states "The future lies ahead." As to the future of the Pacific Rim, it is all a matter of perception. Nations, like people, will disagree and fight. Racism, greed, sexism, waste, and ignorance may threaten the fragile balance between countries. Disease, environmental degradation, and famine could cause pain and agony to thousands. But if the nations of the Pacific Rim can work together to improve their economic and political relationships, the entire region will prosper and the next century will surely be, as Mike Mansfield, U.S. Ambassador to Japan, stated, the "Century of the Pacific."

Challenges for the Future

The greatest challenges facing the nations of the Pacific area, as has been stated earlier, are primarily political, social, and economic in nature. Politically, many nations on the Pacific Rim are moving toward democracy, but will these nations be able to maintain this momentum, or are the changes we have seen just momentary glimpses of political freedom?

Economic prosperity has changed the face of many Pacific Rim cities.

Nationalism is another issue that will affect the future of the Pacific Rim. It can best be summed up in the statement, "My country, right or wrong," and results in people often putting their nation's interests above international interests. For example, many people believe that their own country's products should be bought before a foreign product is bought. American industries advertise with a label that reads, "Made in the U.S.A.," and television stars tell consumers to buy American-made products. There is nothing wrong with purchasing products made in one's own country, but consumers should not be buying products just because they are made in their country. Economics works best when consumers buy the best product at the best price, regardless of where it was manufactured. Otherwise, the result will be inferior and overpriced products that are allowed to survive on the market.

Nationalism also breeds other problems. One of them is known as "dumping." Dumping occurs when a nation allows its businesses to sell vast quantities of a product at an artificially low price in another country. This practice forces the price of the product down and could force some businesses in the affected nation to go bankrupt. As an example, in the 1980s, Japan flooded the U.S. market with microchips. Many U.S. businesses bought these microchips because they were cheaper. This eventually put some U.S. microchip manufacturers out of business.

In the long term, the consequence of this dumping could be disastrous. Since microchips are necessary in the construction of military weapons and other national defense products, the U.S. military would be dependent on a foreign power for its own security. Is it a wise policy for the United States to buy all of its microchips from the Japanese just because the microchips are cheaper? Many senators and representatives felt it was not a good idea, and pressure was put on the Japanese to stop dumping microchips on the U.S. market.

Nationalism also has other repercussions. Many nations on the Pacific Rim are culturally homogeneous, having only one major racial or cultural group. In these countries, foreign products are not considered as desirable as those made locally. For example, Koreans often buy Korean products because products from other countries are not always specifically tailored for the Korean consumer.

But as long as Koreans, Japanese, Canadians, and other Pacific Rim groups make economic decisions based on nationalism rather than on economic logic, the Pacific Rim nations will drift apart rather than be linked together. The Pacific Rim, after all, is an economic unit and depends on economic participation from all its member nations.

In the economic sector, each nation has to meet various challenges. Just as each nation has its own way of thinking, in the same way it plants the seeds for its own difficulties. Japan, long known as a nation where businesses take the ideas of others and improve upon them, has now climbed to the top of the business ladder. Now it must develop its own crop of new products. But can a nation of innovators develop the skills of

Changes are rapidly occurring around the Pacific Rim. In Singapore, both
the old and the new remain.

inventive and creative thought necessary for product development? Can Australia, Canada, and Latin America attract financial investment to stimulate further development of their
resources? Can the United States, with its huge national debt,
solve its deficit problems? Will China, a nation that has traditionally been suspicious of the West, capitalize its system further to make a profit? Will Eastern traditions find fertile soil
in the West? These are difficult questions to answer, but if a
nation wishes to become more prosperous, it will have to
change its attitudes.

The Asian and Southeast Asian Pacific Rim countries are
fortunate in that they do not now have to contend with a high
inflation rate. Most have high rates of productivity. There are
jobs for virtually everyone, and it is reasonable for men or
women to hope that by working hard, they can improve their
lives as well as those of their children. From a national point
of view, the GNP is rising in these countries as is the standard
of living.

In the long run, however, international trade is a system
that cannot be totally controlled. It operates on its own and

has its own laws. If a country tries to adjust those rules, there are economic consequences that could have political repercussions. If a nation tries deficit spending to keep its people happy, it will have inflation. If an automobile company presses its country to raise import taxes, automobiles will cost more and consumers will have fewer dollars to spend on other items.

There are social problems that threaten to upset the delicate interdependence of the Pacific Rim nations. Migration, particularly illegal immigration, is a point of conflict between the United States and Mexico. The border between these two nations is crossed so frequently by illegal immigrants that it is said that the United States no longer has control of its borders.

There are also religious and racial conflicts throughout the Pacific region. They are often of long standing and will take time to resolve. But if they cannot be resolved, the economic links between nations will be weakened. Women being allowed into the work force on an equal footing with men is also a matter of concern. In the United States, legal action has made this possible; in Japan, Korea, Peru, Mexico, and other male-oriented societies, sexual equality may be a long time in coming.

One of the greatest challenges facing nations of the Pacific Rim and the world is the rapid rise in population. With the five billionth human being on earth born in mid-1987, there is no reason to suppose that the population will decline. As a result, there will be more and more people competing for food, clothing, shelter, land, medical attention, and opportunities. Problems like hunger, disease, and war could be the result of too many people and not enough resources. Family planning is controversial in some nations and accepted in others. There is no doubt that the issue of world population will continue to be a major challenge into the next century when the Pacific Rim is projected to have two-thirds of the world's population.

The future of the Pacific Rim is also dependent on the continued presence of immense military forces throughout the region. From an economic standpoint, it usually does not matter which nation has its troops and/or navy present in what areas so long as all areas are covered. The point of having a navy and troops anywhere is to maintain the uninterrupted flow of goods, preserve the peace, and "balance" other military threats. These threats include the presence of the USSR in the Pacific Rim. Specifically the Soviet navy causes concern for Pacific-area democracies because they are not sure why the Soviets are maintaining a presence in the shipping lanes if there are few Soviet transport ships to protect.

On a broader level, one of the benefits for a country maintaining a navy is that country's ability to affect politics in other countries. In areas where political turmoil is common, the presence of a naval force could stop a revolution or, on the other hand, encourage it.

There is also another side to troops and navies. The more troops and navies there are in an area, the greater the chance of conflict, particularly when the two nations are the United States and the Soviet Union. Both nations have large, sophisticated ships, advanced air forces, and hundreds of thousands of troops. These two nations constantly "test" each other's military by having their ships and planes in and around each other's air space and along the 200-mile (320-km) coastal zone. The major problem, however, is not that the United States and the Soviet Union will go to war against each other. The problem is that two other nations might go to war against each other, one nation being supplied by the United States and the other by the Soviets. This was the case in both Korea and Vietnam. These so-called "brush fire wars" are dangerous because they often are long and violent confrontations. If two small nations were to fight each other using only their own resources, the war might end quickly. War is incredibly expensive, and the cost could bankrupt both nations. But with the United States and the Soviet Union each supplying a different side, the ability to continue a war for a long time increases, resulting in many more lives being lost.

Another threat to Pacific Rim nations and the world is terrorism. A small nation or group of fanatics without large military capabilities may wish to antagonize its neighbor or terrorize its citizens. Terrorists are sent to carry out acts of violence. Unfortunately, it is a fairly easy thing to do because most nations have an open door policy in the sense that it is not difficult to get into—or out of—another nation. Palestinian terrorists cross the border into Israel frequently and kill innocent people. Peruvian terrorists, known as members of the "Shining Path," car-bomb Western banks in Lima. All of these so-called "incidents" are acts of war but are considered to be low level by most countries and not serious enough to send a nation into full-scale war. However, continuing incidents of terrorism may force a nation into full-scale civil or international war.

War creates long-term economic difficulties for all nations. The only thing more expensive than losing a war, the old saying goes, is winning one. Someone somewhere is going to have to pay for every war. If the United States and Russia are providing equipment for a war, the United States and Russia are paying the financial costs. But the governments are going to pass the cost along. In the United States, the taxpayers are going to pay that cost. The result is probably deficit spending, which starts the cycle again.

Yet another factor affecting the future of the Pacific Rim is technology. Not only do, as Shakespeare noted, time and tide wait for no man, but technology waits for no person as well. Every day there are technological breakthroughs that

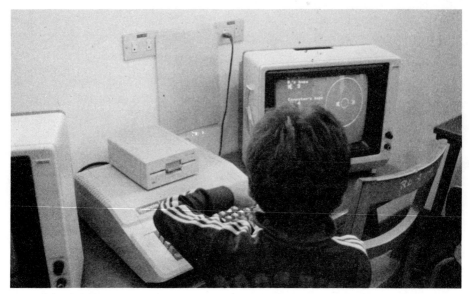

A young person in Peru learns how to use computer technology.

will change the lives of every human on the planet. Technology is increasing communication between individuals at any point on the planet. Computers are becoming more sophisticated and easier to operate. Electrical transmission lines are becoming more efficient. Medical breakthroughs are allowing more children to live and making it easier to live longer. The introduction of new technology into Third World countries is raising their standard of living. Bit by bit, invention by invention, discovery by discovery, the life of humans is being made more complex and possibly easier at the same time.

But there is sometimes a clash between technology and fundamental values and religious beliefs. In the United States there is an ongoing debate on biotechnology, abortion, and birth control. Some religious leaders argue that humankind has no business involving itself with God's work. Other religious leaders say that humans must resolve their own destiny and not wait for God to act. In other parts of the world, to die in the pursuit of a holy or political cause is a noble enterprise.

But as technological advances increase lifespan, there are still factors that work against this forward movement. As more and more diseases are cured, other diseases appear. The greatest threat to the health of humankind currently appears to be AIDS, Acquired Immune Deficiency Syndrome. AIDS is a blood or sexually transmitted disease that attacks the body's immune system. A healthy human body can fight off diseases because it has a defense system that keeps the body healthy. But AIDS kills off the defense cells, leaving the body helpless to any disease that the body may contract.

AIDS is a dangerous disease for two reasons. First, there is, as yet, no cure. Second, without major changes in the sexual attitudes of people around the globe, AIDS cannot be stopped. It strikes people of all races and religions in all countries. In some parts of Africa, AIDS is so widespread that villages, which have existed since the dawn of time, may be wiped out in one generation.

There is also the very real fear that AIDS could do to the modern world what the Black Plague did to Europe in the fourteenth century. In that era, it was conceivable that the European population might disappear as a result of the plague. Today, the cost of AIDS in terms of human lives is staggering, and its cost in terms of money is also staggering. Every AIDS patient requires hospital care. In the United States, it is estimated that every AIDS patient will cost the U.S. taxpayers $100,000. The more AIDS patients there are, the higher the cost to the nation.

Regardless of the language, religion, culture, economic base, and race or political inclination of the countries in the Pacific Rim, the region is an interdependent unit. Language

Bamboo scaffolding here in Macao is one symbol of progress found in the
Asia Pacific region.

barriers continue to decrease. Racism is slowly fading, but nationalism may be a difficult concept to control. In the final analysis, all nations of the Pacific Rim are in the same boat, so to speak, and when one end is rocked, the other dips. The fate of all nations depends on the well-being of each individual nation. The mutual benefits that Pacific Rim nations can enjoy keep them working together for the good of all. That is the road map for the future, making the next one hundred years indeed the "Century of the Pacific."

Appendix

COMPARATIVE DATA ON SELECTED NATIONS AND TERRITORIES
IN THE PACIFIC RIM

NATIONS	Area in sq. mi (sq. km)	Population (1987 est.)	Population (per sq. mi)	GNP	Name of Currency
Australia	2,966,150 (7,682,300)	16,200,000	6	166.2	Australian Dollar
Brunei	2,226 (5,765)	200,000	98	4.4	Brunei Dollar
Cambodia	69,884 (181,000)	6,500,000	93	.5	Riel
Canada	3,851,809 (9,976,186)	25,900,000	7	335	Canadian Dollar
Chile	292,132 (756,622)	12,400,000	42	22.6	Peso
China	3,691,521 (9,561,000)	1,062,000,000	288	343	Yuan
Colombia	455,355 (1,179,369)	29,900,000	66	29	Peso
Costa Rica	19,652 (50,898)	2,800,000	143	3.5	Colón
Ecuador	109,484 (270,670)	10,000,000	91	11.9	Sucre
El Salvador	8,260 (21,393)	5,300,000	642	3.8	Colón
Fiji	7,078 (18,333)	700,000	99	1.25	Fijian Dollar
Guatemala	42,042 (108,889)	8,400,000	205	9.1	Quetzal
Honduras	43,277 (112,088)	4,700,000	109	2.9	Lempira
Indonesia	735,268 (1,904,344)	174,900,000	238	90.3	Rupiah
Japan	143,574 (371,857)	122,200,000	851	1,233	Yen

COMPARATIVE DATA ON SELECTED NATIONS AND TERRITORIES
IN THE PACIFIC RIM

NATIONS	Area in sq. mi (sq. km)	Population (1987 est.)	Population (per sq. mi)	GNP	Name of Currency
Kiribati	264 (683)	62,000	235	30 million	Australian Dollar
Korea(North)	46,768 (121,129)	21,400,000	458	23	Won
Korea(South)	38,031 (98,500)	42,100,000	1,107	90.6	Won
Malaysia	128,328 (332,370)	16,100,000	125	28.4	Ringgit
Mexico	761,600 (1,972,547)	81,900,000	108	168	Peso
Nauru	8 (21)	8,000	976	160 million	Australian Dollar
New Zealand	103,884 (269,062)	3,300,000	32	18.9	New Zealand Dollar
Nicaragua	50,180 (130,000)	3,500,000	70	2.4	Cordoba
Panama	29,761 (77,082)	2,300,000	74	4.2	Balboa
Papua New Guinea	178,704 (462,840)	3,600,000	20	2	Kina
Peru	496,222 (1,285,216)	20,700,000	42	17.9	Inti
Philippines	115,830 (300,000)	61,500,000	531	32	Peso
Singapore	240 (622)	2,600,000	10,924	18.4	Singapore Dollar
Solomon Islands	11,500 (29,785)	300,000	26	160 million	Solomon Islands Dollar
Taiwan (Republic of China)	13,895 (35,988)	19,600,000	1,411	60	New Taiwan Dollar

COMPARATIVE DATA ON SELECTED NATIONS AND TERRITORIES
IN THE PACIFIC RIM

NATIONS	Area in sq. mi (sq. km)	Population (1987 est.)	Population (per sq. mi)	GNP	Name of Currency
Thailand	198,455 (514,000)	53,600,000	270	52.4	Baht
Tonga	290 (751)	107,000	369	65 million	Pa'anga
Tuvalu	10 (26)	8,000	700	4 million	Australian Dollar
USSR	8,649,489 (22,402,200)	284,000,000	32	2,062	Ruble
United States	3,540,939 (9,171,032)	243,800,000	69	4,206	U.S. Dollar
Vanuatu	5,700 (14,763)	200,000	18	63 million	Vatu
Vietnam	127,246 (329,566)	62,200,000	489	9.8	Dong
Western Samoa	1,093 (2,831)	200,000	183	130 million	Tala

Territories Etc.

French Polynesia	1,544 (4,000)	200,000	130	1.3	Pacific Financial Community Franc
Hong Kong	398 (1,031)	5,600,000	14,322	21.5	Hong Kong Dollar
Macao	6 (15.5)	400,000	66,667	550 million	Pataca
New Caledonia &Dependencies	7,374 (19,103)	200,000	27	1.1	Pacific Financial Community Franc

Glossary

ABORIGINE—the native people in a region.

ACCULTURATION—changing of a culture due to contact with another culture.

ASSOCIATION OF SOUTHEAST ASIAN NATIONS (ASEAN)—an organization of nations composed of Thailand, Singapore, Indonesia, Malaysia, Brunei, and the Philippines.

ATOLL—ringlike islands created by volcanic action or coral growth.

CATACLYSMIC CHANGE—geological change that occurs quickly and often violently, like an earthquake.

COMMODITY—a useful good that can be traded.

CONSULATE—a mission to a foreign nation that is lower ranking than an embassy.

COUP D'ETAT—the rapid overthrow of a government.

CULTURAL ASSIMILATION—a process in which people borrow ideas from another culture and use them in their own culture.

DEFICIT—a situation in which more money is spent than is possessed.

DEFICIT SPENDING—a nation's spending of more money than it has or is earning.

DIALECT—a regional variety of a spoken language.

DUMPING—selling a great number of products in a foreign market at a reduced price.

EMBASSY—the highest mission to a foreign government, headed by an ambassador.

EXPORT—selling or trading of goods and services to other nations.

GRADATIONAL CHANGE—geological change that occurs over a long period of time, like erosion.

GREAT-CIRCLE ROUTE—the shortest flying route between cities. Best determined by use of a globe.

GROSS NATIONAL PRODUCT (GNP)—a nation's total output of goods and services.

HEGEMONY—a league of states with equal votes in which one becomes a dominant leader because of its power and influence.

IMPERIALISM—a system of establishing colonies, often by force, to build an empire.

IMPORT—bringing in goods and services from another nation by trading or buying.

INCENDIARY BOMB—a weapon designed to cause fire.

LINGUA FRANCA—the commercial language of a nation, not a local dialect.

MESTIZO—a person of mixed blood who in Latin America has American Indian and European ancestry.

NATIONALIZATION—a policy of taking over industries by the government of a nation.

NEWLY INDUSTRIALIZED COUNTRIES (NICs)—nations that have become industrialized since the late 1960s.

PER CAPITA INCOME—the average amount of money earned by a person over the course of a year.

PLATE TECTONICS—changes in the earth's crust caused by plate movements.

SOUTHEAST ASIA TREATY ORGANIZATION (SEATO)—a defense organization created in 1954 with members including Australia, France, Great Britain, New Zealand, Pakistan, the Philippines, Thailand, and the United States. The organization dissolved in 1977.

STANDARD OF LIVING—a statistic reflecting the average level of purchasing power available to a citizen of a nation.

TARIFF—a tax levied by a government on imported or exported goods or services.

TELECOMMUNICATION—communication conducted by transmission of electronic signals.

TRADE WAR—a confrontation in which two or more nations use weapons like boycotts, tariffs, or laws to wage an economic war.

Further Reading

Bauer, E.E. *China Takes Off: Technology Transfer and Modernization.* Seattle, Washington: University of Washington Press, 1986.

Benjamin, Roger, and Kudrle, Robert T.; Editors. *The Industrial Future of the Pacific Basin.* Boulder, Colorado: Westview Press, 1984.

Black, Jan Knippers. *Latin America, Its Problems and Its Promise.* Boulder, Colorado: Westview Press, 1984.

Bryant, Adam. *Canada, Good Neighbor to the World.* Minneapolis, Minnesota: Dillon Press, 1987.

Bumsted, J.M. *Interpreting Canada's Past.* Toronto: Oxford University Press, 1986.

Burns, E. Bradford. *Latin America: A Concise Interpretative History.* Englewood Cliffs, New Jersey: Prentice-Hall, 1986.

Cortes Conde, Roberto. *The Latin American Economies: Growth and the Export Sector.* New York: Holmes and Meier, 1985.

Davidson, Judith. *Japan, Where East Meets West.* Minneapolis, Minnesota: Dillon Press, 1983.

Dostert, Pierre Etienne. *Latin America 1988.* Washington, D.C.: Stryker-Post Publications, 1988. (Updated annually).

Drysdale, John. *Singapore: Struggle for Success.* Singapore: Times Books, 1984.

Fukutake, Tadashi. *Japanese Society Today.* Tokyo: University of Tokyo Press, 1982.

Fox, William T.R. *A Continent Apart: The United States and Canada in World Politics.* Toronto and Buffalo: University of Toronto Press, 1985.

Franko, Lawrence G. *The Threat of Japanese Multinationals*. New York: John Wiley, 1983.

Granatstein, J.L. *Twentieth Century Canada*. Toronto: McGraw-Hill Ryerson, 1986.

Graupp, Patrick. *The Life of John Japanese: Working in Japan*. New York: Vantage Press, 1985.

Hinton, Harold C. *East Asia and the Western Pacific 1988*. Washington, D.C.: Stryker-Post Publications, 1988. (Updated annually).

Hofheinz, Roy, and Calder, Kent E. *The Eastasia Edge*. New York: Basic Books, 1982.

Johnson, Chalmers. *MITI and the Japanese Miracle*. Stanford, California: Stanford University Press, 1982.

Knight, Bill; Editor. *Hong Kong 1986*. Hong Kong: Government Information Services, 1986.

Kuo, Shirley W.Y. *The Taiwan Economy in Transition*. Boulder, Colorado: Westview, 1983.

Linder, Staffan Burenstam. *The Pacific Century: Economic and Political Consequences of the Asian-Pacific Dynamism*. Stanford, California: Stanford University Press, 1986.

Malcolm, Andrew H. *The Canadians*. Toronto and New York: Bantam Books, 1986.

McCreary, Don R. *Japanese-U.S. Business Negotiations: A Cross Cultural Study*. New York: Praeger, 1986.

McMullen, Neil. *The Newly Industrializing Countries: Adjusting to Success*. Washington, D.C.: National Planning Association, 1984.

Morley, James W.; Editor. *The Pacific Basin: New Challenges for the United States*. New York: The Academy of Political Science, 1986.

National Identity Office. *Thailand in the 80s*. Bangkok: Muang Boran Publishing House, 1984.

Osborne, Milton. *Southeast Asia*. Boston: George Allen & Unwin Inc., 1985.

Quo, F.Q.; Editor. *Politics of the Pacific Nations.* Boulder, Colorado: Westview, 1983.

Robertson, Dougal. *Survive the Savage Sea*. Lercestershire: Ulverscroft, 1986.

Salisbury, Harrison Evans. *China: 100 Years of Revolution*. New York: Holt, Rinehart, and Winston, 1983.

Shoemaker, M. Wesley. *The Soviet Union and Eastern Europe 1988*. Washington, D.C.: Stryker-Post Publications, 1988. (Updated annually).

Suryadinata, Leo. *China and the ASEAN States: The Ethnic Chinese Dimension*. Singapore: Singapore University Press, 1985.

Terrill, Ross. *The Australians*. New York: Simon and Schuster, 1987.

Thompson, Wayne C. *Canada 1988*. Washington, D.C.: Stryker-Post Publications, 1988. (Updated annually).

Time-Life Books. *China*. Amsterdam: Time-Life Books, 1984.

Time-Life Books. *Japan*. Alexandria, Virginia: Time-Life Books, 1985.

Uchino, Tatsuro. *Japan's Postwar Economy: An Insider's View of Its History and Its Future*. Tokyo; New York: Kodansha International, 1983.

Vlahos, Olivia. *Far Eastern Beginnings*. New York: Viking Press, 1976.

Woronoff, Jon. *Asia's "Miracle" Economies*. Tokyo: Lotus Press, 1986.

Woronoff, Jon. *Inside Japan, Inc*. Tokyo: Lotus Press, 1982.

Woronoff, Jon. *Korea's Economy, Man-Made Miracle*. Seoul: Si-sa-yong-o-sa Publishers, 1983.

Zagoria, D.S.; Editor. *Soviet Policy in East Asia*. New Haven, Connecticut: Yale University Press, 1982.

Index

tariff, 71, 113-114
taxes, 88, 113, 135, 137, 139
technology, 25, 37, 98-100, 137, *138,* 139
telecommunications, 99-101
telex, 99
terrorism, 137
Thailand, 9, 11, 20, *23, 55,* 57, *87,* 91, 106, 130, 145
Third World, 123, 138
time zones, 14
Tokyo, 14, 16, 85
Tonga, 10, 57, 145
tort reform, 122
trade war, 113-114, 116
transportation, 82, 98-100, *101*
Treaty of Portsmouth, 69
Truman, Harry, 73
Tuvalu, 10, 57, 145

U

United Nations, 89-90
United States, 9, 21-26, 50-53, 57-60, 61-76, 89, 94, 98, 101, 104, 106, 108-109, 123, 125, 135, 139, 145
economy, 53, 61-63, 70-72, 74-76, 78, 80-82, 97, 116-123, 132-133, 145
military, 24-25, 42, 61-64, 66-70, 72-74, 84-85, 90, 104-105, *112,* 126, *127,* 128, 133, 136-137
trade, 24-26, 41-42, 84, 91, 94-95, 106, *107*
World War II, 25, 61-64, 112-114, *115,* 116, 123
U.S.S. Missouri, 61, *63*

V

Vancouver, 14, *51,* 85
Vanuatu, 10, 145
Vietnam, 9, 21, 55, 85, 98, 112, 123, 127-128, 130, 145
Vietnam War, 114, *115,* 127-128, 136
Vikings, 29
volcanoes, 17-19

W

Western Samoa, 10, 145
World Bank, 123
World War I, 70, 112
World War II, 25, 61-63, 79-80, 89, 112-114, 116, 123, 126

Y

Yellow Peril, 69-70

About the Authors

Douglas A. Phillips is a leader in the movement to educate young people about the Pacific Rim. As an advocate for Pacific Rim studies he has given presentations, written articles, and traveled extensively in that area. He earned his B.S. and M.S. in education at Northern State College in South Dakota. He now works as the social studies program coordinator for a large school district in Alaska.

Steven C. Levi is a freelance writer and small business consultant in Alaska. His published titles range in subject from scholarly history to poetry. He has a B.A. in ancient history from the University of California at Davis and an M.A. in American history from San Jose State College.